# PRAISE FOR
# WORKING MOM'S 411

As CEO of a corporation and mother to two grown children, I related to the challenges addressed in *Working Mom's 411*. I only wish it had been released *before* my kids were grown!

## Dianna Booher

CEO, Booher Consultants and author of *Ten Smart Moves for Women Who Want to Succeed in Love and Life*

Full of tips and advice, this is a must-have companion for working moms. Michelle LaRowe has managed to make it more than worth-while to take time from your busy life to read this book.

## Samantha Ettus

Mother of two and creator of *The Experts' Guide to the Baby Years*

*Working Mom's 411* is a much-needed addition to any working mom's bookshelf. Michelle LaRowe offers practical tips and advice as she shares her wisdom on how to balance kids, career and home.

## Suzanne Hansen

Mother of two and author of *New York Times* bestseller *You'll Never Nanny in this Town Again! The True Adventures of a Hollywood Nanny*

As a full-time mom, teacher and pastor's wife, I appreciate the wit, wisdom and practical ideas that Michelle LaRowe offers in *Working Mom's 411*. This book is vital for any mom trying to do it all!

## Lauri Hawley

Mom to three, Faith Assembly of God, Hyannis, MA

Michelle LaRowe does it again! Filled with solid advice and practical tips, *Working Mom's 411* is a must-read for mothers who are looking for effective strategies on how to manage work and home.

## Stella Reid

Wife and stepmom, Nanny Stella on *Nanny 911* and author of *Nanny 911*

Michelle LaRowe

# WORKING MOM'S 411

How to Manage    Kids    Career    & Home

**Regal**

From Gospel Light
Ventura, California, U.S.A.

Published by Regal
From Gospel Light
Ventura, California, U.S.A.
*www.regalbooks.com*
Printed in the U.S.A.

Published in association with the literary agency of WordServe Literary Group, Ltd.,
10152 S. Knoll Circle, Highlands Ranch, CO 80130

Library of Congress Cataloging-in-Publication Data
LaRowe, Michelle R.
Working mom's 411 : how to manage kids, career, and home / Michelle LaRowe.
p. cm.
ISBN 978-0-8307-4608-8 (trade paper)
1. Working mothers. 2. Children of working parents. 3. Work and family. I. Title.
HQ759.48.L375 2009
649'.1—dc22
2008037996

1 2 3 4 5 6 7 8 9 10 11 12 13 14 15 / 15 14 13 12 11 10 09

Rights for publishing this book outside the U.S.A. or in non-English languages are
administered by Gospel Light Worldwide, an international not-for-profit ministry.
For additional information, please visit www.glww.org, email info@glww.org, or write
to Gospel Light Worldwide, 1957 Eastman Avenue, Ventura, CA 93003, U.S.A.

*To my working single mom,*
*who taught me that with God, anything is possible.*

# CONTENTS

## SECTION 1:
## What to Expect (from Your Boss and Your Body!) When You're Expecting

## SECTION 2:
## Mixing Babies with Business

## SECTION 3:
## Of Crayons and Careers

# ACKNOWLEDGMENTS

*To my husband, Jeff*—Without your love, support, understanding and undying patience, I would not have been able to complete this book, or survive the first trimester of pregnancy.

*To Greg and Becky Johnson*—Your agenting and editing talents are unsurpassed! The commitment and dedication you give to each and every client and project make things come together flawlessly. I cannot say enough good things about the two of you. You are certainly one amazing team.

*To the folks at Regal*—Thank you for the warm welcome into your publishing family and for your dedication to this project.

*To Kim Bangs*—Your input and advice helped shape this book and has helped me learn to connect with my readers in a deeper way.

*To all my friends and family*—Thanks for always being supportive and encouraging me and all my endeavors.

*To Him*—I thank God that He has given me the opportunity to give back to others what He has given to me. He's opened doors that no man could open.

# INTRODUCTION

Our eyes first met on an early May morning in 1995—Sue, a first-time mother, and I, interviewing for a job to help pay my way through the spring semester at Bridgewater State College, where I was finishing up my degree in chemistry (of all things). Sue was searching for a nanny to care for her twin infant girls, Kayla and Alicia, so that she could return to her post as resident social worker for a community nursing home.

We were both nervous, strangers meeting for the first time, sitting on the dusty rose-colored couch in her home. At the time, I was too naive to realize that Sue was much more nervous than I: She was about to place her precious new lives in a stranger's hands.

The two-page printout of my professional-looking résumé—consisting of references from years of babysitting, posh summer nanny positions for stay-at-home moms and a delivery job at a Chinese restaurant—was the only real formality in the interview. Mostly, our time together was spent "oohing" and "ahhing" over her two, still new, sweet bundles of joy. (Alas, some things never change! Melting around such cuteness, fresh from heaven, will always be part of my modus operandi.)

Nearly 13 years have gone by since I first worked for Sue, but to this day, when she runs into my mom at our hometown grocery store, she asks the same question: "Can you believe it all started with us?"

Little did we know that this "interview" would begin my more than decade-old love affair with the nanny profession, working mothers, and advocacy for quality in-home childcare.

## More Than My Job

Being a nanny has always been more than a job to me. It's my passion. Providing quality, loving childcare—always for twins (and now twins alongside their older siblings)—is what I am about.

Educating parents and the public on the importance of high-quality childcare is another passion of mine. Over the years, I have served as president of Boston Area Nannies, vice president of the International Nanny Association, and have held memberships in various nanny organizations, including a group called Christian Nannies. Through these organizations, I've had a voice (okay, a loud voice for those who know me and my, um . . . thick Boston accent) in advocating for quality in-home childcare and educating parents about how to find (and keep!) it.

Since I was awarded the 2004 International Nanny Association Nanny of the Year Award, the avenue for my voice has changed. I've been fortunate to expand my career through writing parenting books and articles, and to launch a parenting consulting business for working moms and working moms-to-be (check it out at www.michellelarowe.com). It's been so rewarding to work one on one with women who feel like there is no possible way to make this working-mom thing work, only to see them transformed into lean, mean, working-mother machines. As one of my clients put it, "If I had known half of what Michelle knows about navigating the path of working motherhood *before* I gave birth, I would have had a much more peaceful pregnancy and felt much more prepared and confident about how I was going to handle my new dual role."

## Working with a Working Mom

It didn't take long for me to realize that when I signed up to be a nanny for a working mother, I was signing on for more than a job. I was committing to be a vital part of her support system that would allow her to be the best at both of her roles: full-time mother and full-time career woman.

Over the years that I've worked alongside working mothers, I have come to learn something about myself: There is an alter ego sharing the heart and mind of this modern-day Mary Poppins.

It's the intense, type-A, lover of all things organizational (I brake for the Container Store!) personality that derives *huge* gratification from knowing that when I do my job well, my employer can do her job well on both the work and the home fronts.

Now don't get me wrong—there are few things I love more than being greeted first thing on a Monday morning by a newly walking one-year-old who wobbles over in pure excitement, arms in the air, ready to be swept up in my embrace. But there's something almost equally satisfying about the buzz of joy I feel when my employer, a high-powered executive at a Fortune 500 company, says to me as she races behind her toddler, "I don't know how you do it."

Oh, let me count the ways. And one day, I actually did. As I began to jot down my best tips and tricks, they eventually developed into this book, which I am now delighted to share with working moms across the country!

## What Can *You* Learn from *Me*?

Let me just say that this book is all about *you,* today's working mother. But before we dive into the tips and tricks of successfully managing kids, career and home, you need to know a few things about me . . . and why a newlywed with her firstborn in diapers has anything to say to you about, of all things, working motherhood.

As a professional nanny with more than a decade of experience in dual-income homes, my heart has ached as I've seen the struggle working mothers face as they try to do it all. The stress that comes with having to choose between family dinners and business meetings, with attempting to coordinate childcare coverage and with the daily struggle of not being able to be in multiple places at the same time can truly be overwhelming.

But I've also seen their stress begin to fade and the pieces fall into place as I've helped guide them toward a life of balancing a happy family with a rewarding career. And often all it takes is a little help, a practical system and a guilt-reduced insight into their Supermom life.

I have counseled mothers like Stacey who stayed home but was itching to get back to work, and mothers like Hope, who had to work but was desperate to stay home. For these mothers, and for many others like them, I came up with a personal, practical "how to balance work and home" plan that included creative suggestions (along with helpful tips) to guide them toward getting more of what they really wanted into their days, every day.

Chances are, if you are holding this book, you've either been trying to do it all or are getting ready to do it all and want to know how you'll ever manage. Either way, I'm here to help.

## How This Book Will Help You

My years of dedication to empowering working mothers and my deep commitment to providing the highest quality of childcare to their children have provided much inspiration for *Working Mom's 411*. Most of what you'll read here is based on my first-hand experiences, my successes and my occasional failures as I learned what worked and what didn't to help working moms find the best in both worlds: family and career.

If you take to heart my tried-and-true solutions to the most common dilemmas that working mothers face, you'll be walking the home/work balance beam like a gold medal Olympian in no time. Okay, maybe I am promising a bit too much . . . even Cătălina Ponor takes a tumble now and again, but she always gets up, regains her composure and tries again. I promise I'll show you how (and gently encourage you) to do the same.

*Working Mom's 411* seemed to be the natural sequel to the two books I wrote for parents in the *Nanny to the Rescue!* series. While the previous books focused on managing your kids and their behavior, this one is about managing oh so much more.

Whether you're struggling with the guilt of missing your child's first steps, choosing quality childcare, feeling overwhelmed with scheduling demands, balancing work, marriage and kids, or trying to stay connected to the world of soccer moms, *Working Mom's 411* will give you time-saving tips and practical strategies to solve the working mother's most pressing dilemmas.

So how can today's working mother balance a loving home life with a productive work life? Take off your leather pumps, put on your comfy slippers, put your feet up and turn the page. Let the learning begin!

# SECTION 1

---

## WHAT TO EXPECT
## (FROM YOUR BOSS AND YOUR BODY!)
## WHEN YOU'RE EXPECTING

# THE MOTHER LOAD

## SCENE 1: TAKE 1
### *Baby's Dedication*

**Aunt Claire** (*to Aunt Missy, in an irritated tone*): Can you believe she's going back to work? Why have kids if you are going to have someone else take care of them?

**Aunt Missy**: That's kind of a harsh thing to say, don't you think? It's tough for young parents to make it on one income these days.

**Aunt Claire** (*snippily*): Oh, don't even go there. She *wants* to work.

**Aunt Missy**: Whoa. You are making it sound like her decision to work means she is a bad mother. You know, besides the fact that their family may actually need the extra income, she may want to use that degree she worked four years to earn! She may find meaning in her career that helps her be a better mother. I know I was a lot happier at home when I got out of the house and worked part-time. Back in the old days, women usually had generations of aunts and grandmas living nearby who could give moms regular breaks from their children. Parents helped young couples get a start in life, often by donating a piece of the family farm to them and helping them build their homestead, complete with a community barn-raising.

Don't be so critical when you don't know the whole situation. Your choice may be right for you, but it doesn't mean it's necessarily right for everyone. Couples don't have an easy row to hoe these days with families so mobile and far apart.

**Aunt Claire** (*nervously, afraid she's been overheard*): Shhhh. She's coming. . . . Quiet. (*to the young mother, feigning joy*) Congratulations! What a beautiful baby girl!

Whether you have been the subject of such a conversation or not, the truth is that this controversial dialogue has occurred millions of times and has deeply affected mothers from all walks of life. From the executive CEO of a Fortune 500 company to the retail sales clerk at your local TJ Maxx, working women are often caught in the cross-fire as the war between working and stay-at-home moms continues to rage. Struggling with deep-seated emotions and black and white ideas about what's best for everyone, today's mothers are often made to feel guilty if they are, for whatever reason, a part of the paid workforce.

## Rooted Deep

For many mothers, the struggle between working and staying at home comes down to much more than a financial decision. Although finances are often the most common denominator in the final decision to return to work, emotions, family history, personal convictions and personality all play a role in the decision-making process. Taking a good look at each of these can provide moms with much-needed insight into how they are really feeling and can help to make the decision much easier.

Stop for a moment and consider your childhood. Did both of your parents work? With whom did you spend your childhood? Who were the most influential people during your formative years? How do you envision your ideal family life? What emotions does the term "working mother" evoke in you? What does your career mean to you? Can you imagine yourself not working?

Answering these questions will give you insight into your own feelings about returning to work, and you'll quickly realize that for every mom, sorting through these emotions is more complex than you ever may have thought.

Take Kellie, for example. She grew up in a home where her mother worked full time. She resented being a latch-key kid, so she vowed never to work when she had kids of her own, and she didn't. Her personal experience and the emotions that accompanied her memories of feeling neglected and lonely predetermined her parenting plan of action.

Sherry, on the other hand, has always admired her mother's ability to juggle a job and a home life and has decided that her kids will grow up happy and resilient if she also works.

Then there's Bethany, who had painful memories of her parents' constant struggle with poverty. Bethany's mom, though loving, felt stuck in a marriage to an abusive husband, but she had no means of supporting herself and her children—which led her to feel that she was unable to escape. As you can imagine, Bethany made her own childhood vow never to end up in her mother's shoes. She'd always work, at least part-time, and keep her résumé current so that she'd never feel powerless should life circumstances require her to step into the role of primary breadwinner.

It's no wonder the debate between mothers who stay at home and mothers who work often becomes so heated. The so-called

Mommy Wars are fuelled by intense emotions and work under the presumption that "I know best," as one person transfers her attitudes and expectations (based on her own personal experiences) on to another. If motherhood were only a one-size-fits-all mold, there would be no debate.

Let me say this up front: Only *you* can decide what's right for you and yours. Only you will know if you can live with the sometimes ambivalent emotions that accompany the choice to return to work. As a working mother, you'll have to accept that you may hear of your baby's first tooth from the babysitter or nanny, rather than actually seeing it emerge for yourself. You'll have to learn to be okay with someone else giving you daily updates on your own child. And of course, you'll need a backup plan that allows you to rush home when the sitter gets sick.

The mere thought of these scenarios may be enough to cause a lump to swell up in the back of your throat, but take heart: These intense feelings are normal. Recognizing the emotional pull on your heartstrings and learning to separate your feelings from facts will become your greatest asset as a working mother.

Think about your child's first ear infection. Do you think your geographic locale dictated the intensity of heartache that you felt for your ailing child? Of course not! As a working mom, you probably felt bad that you weren't the one to identify the first sign of illness—or that you weren't the one giving your child her daily dose of medication. But did your being at work contribute to the infection? No. Did your continuing to work prevent it from going away? No. Remember, at the end of the day, if you've carefully chosen a loving, trustworthy caregiver, and she and your child have bonded, then you *have* taken care of your child.

Every mom will feel for her child's pain, whether or not she works outside of the home. And almost every mom would prefer to be the one at home, caring for her child during an illness. But life is complicated, and many moms aren't able to be home with their children. However, the great news is that children are amazingly resilient and responsive to trusted caregivers.

As a working mom, you've got to be smart with your heart. Stop and think before you let yourself be drawn into the Perpetual Guilt Trap. Is giving your child PB&J in the car (because you didn't have time to make him a proper breakfast before school) really going to cause him to fail his spelling test? (Actually, PB&J with a glass of milk makes for a pretty nutritious breakfast!)

Recognize that both stay-at-home moms and working moms struggle with difficult choices. When Connor's T-ball game, Jeff's baseball game *and* Jenna's dance recital all occur on the same day, *any* and *every* mom is going to feel stretched and conflicted. Working moms do not have the market cornered when it comes to guilt trips. These come with the territory for every mom—whether she works outside of the home or not—at some time or another. So rest assured that lots of your worries are "mommy-versal."

When a parent cannot be all things at all times to her children, real benefits are often the result. A working mom gives her children the opportunity to learn independence and resourcefulness. Further, as children learn self-sufficiency, their pride in their accomplishments also increases. If you don't get home in time to cook supper and the kids have to get creative with what's in the fridge, they may just discover that they're pretty handy in the kitchen. Who knows how many Food Network stars were born in kitchens where they were allowed to cook and experiment and create meals from what was on hand? If your children learn to wash and fold their own laundry or help with other household chores, they may fuss for the moment, but at the end of the day, they'll be well prepared for life out in the real world.

## Family Finances

For many families, finances are the main reason that Mom returns to work. My heart goes out to those moms who do not have the luxury of choice, the moms whose circumstances have made a clear-cut decision for them.

In families where Mom is the primary breadwinner, she carries the added stress of *literally* having to do it all. In homes headed by single mothers, Mom is often missing not only the financial support from a spouse, but also that all-important emotional connection. Creating a solid support system can help ease the emotional burden that comes with being a single working mom (keep reading, single moms, the next chapter is just for you!).

Some families may not *need* a dual income to survive, but a second income is desirable in order to enjoy some of life's extras. And the trade-off—for everyone—is worth it. It's the reason that pizza night (or sushi, for some!) can happen, not to mention special family vacations. When a child shows that she has talent in a particular area, many moms return to work part-time to help pay for riding lessons or hockey equipment, or to buy their budding Mozart a good musical instrument and lessons, or to send their "Meryl Streep in the making" to drama camp. Only you, your kids and your mate (if there's one in the picture) can decide when and how much of a trade-off you're willing to make. And as your kids get older, it can be wise to have a family discussion on the benefits of mom working as you gently remind them why Mom isn't always home when school gets out.

Remind yourself, too, that by working outside of the home, you are contributing tangible love to the family, even though you may not be there every minute they'd like you to be around. Though you may miss a couple of their soccer games because of work obligations, your income is paying for your children's sports-related expenses so that they *can* play!

## More Than a Paycheck

Maybe you've spent years climbing the corporate ladder or put in years of schooling to fulfill your childhood dream of becoming a professional. Or maybe you've worked hard to break through the "glass ceiling" and finally landed that position that fits you perfectly—like Cinderella's glass slipper. Perhaps you are just gifted in special ways and your job allows you to use those gifts in ways additional to motherhood. I know a few fabulous teachers who feel that if they had stopped teaching to stay home full time, they would have turned their back on one of their major life callings. It's not that they don't want to mother; they want to be a loving mom *and* a great teacher. Or doctor. Or CEO.

Does the thought of trading your briefcase for a full-time diaper bag make you feel a bit "poopy" yourself? If so, you may already understand the significant role your work plays in your emotional health. A research study conducted by Abigail Tuttle O'Keeffe titled "It's Not What Mothers Do But the 'Reasons' That They Do It: Maternal Reasons for Employment Decisions and Mothers' Well-Being"[1] cited personal fulfillment, along with financial reasons, as the two leading determining factors for returning to work.

Many working moms truly enjoy their work. They are enriched by their daily interactions with other adults and the positive feelings of self-worth that they receive at the workplace. Working moms often feel a sense of accomplishment as a result of the contributions that they make in their fields, as well as the financial contributions that they make to their families. And as the old saying goes, "If mama ain't happy, ain't nobody happy."

Certainly, if given the choice, most kids would rather have a happy, fulfilled mother than a depressed, bored one—even if it means having her away from home a few more hours each day. So if you are one of those women who is simply at your emotional best when you've got a job you enjoy, your children will pick up on your life-loving attitude. Kids really do want happy, fulfilled parents—and as long as the time you spend with your family is positive, it will overcome lots of the negatives that come with working outside of the home.

## Not Guilty!

The sun is barely shining, and you already know it's going to be one of those days. Jack is pouting because he wants the French toast that you promised him for breakfast, and you are out of eggs. The phone rings. Your nanny is sick, and you are now left scrambling for coverage. You sort things out and find a sub; the kids are crying but cared for. You grab your coffee and head out the door, a half hour late. As you turn the corner into the parking lot at the office, your coffee turns, too—down the front of your white blouse. *What was I thinking, going back to work?* you wonder. Staying home would have been so much easier, but then again, you wanted to return to work. Still, at times like this you are overwhelmed by feelings of guilt and sadness because of your decision.

As I've mentioned, guilt is the number one negative emotion working mothers seem to struggle with. Their guilt is often a result of feeling responsible for their child's every failure, heartache or let down. Recognize that even if you were home, you'd still struggle with guilt—either because you can't afford tuba lessons for your child or because she tripped over the vacuum cord that you forgot to put away. Remember that just because you feel guilty, it doesn't mean you *are* guilty. Working parents and stay-at-home parents are both guaranteed to experience guilt, what Erma Bombeck called the "gift that keeps on giving." For better or worse, parenting and guilt seem to go hand in hand.

Deciding to return to work is a personal family decision. And, if you are happy with your decision, your family will generally be happy, too.

## Reconciling Your Heart

On any average day, you may experience a spectrum of emotions ranging from guilt to giddiness, anxiety to accomplishment. This flux of feelings is absolutely normal.

So how can you tackle the intense emotions that come with balancing work and family? Working mothers agree that the key to successfully managing these feelings is twofold. First, you've got to secure quality childcare, finding just the right match for your particular child's needs. Second, you've got to build a great support system.

When you have confidence in your childcare arrangement, it's much easier to go to work, even if your child fusses at the initial separation (partings are, after all, as Shakespeare noted, "such sweet sorrow"). Although you'd rather be the one to comfort your child, if you trust your caregiver, you can calm your ruffled feelings with the knowledge that your child will be lovingly soothed and redirected and that he or she will soon be playing contentedly. Ideally, you can also call your caregiver to check in on your child on your way to work, just to make sure things have settled down. Ninety-nine percent of the time, once you are out the door, a skilled nanny or babysitter can get your child soothed and refocused in very little time.

Having a support system in place—a friend who can lend an ear for phone conversations (or who has a knack for empathetic emailing), a prayer partner or a supportive sister—can help you feel balanced, especially if she's been where you are! Knowing that you have someone who is concerned about what you are going through, who can affirm you when you're feeling down and who can listen without giving unsolicited advice can help stop the emotional roller coaster and help you to find your bearings again.

## Expectation Modification

One of the most challenging aspects of being a working mom is managing expectations—both yours and those of others. Working motherhood is a world of compromise, flexibility and negotiation. It's a balancing act between doing what you want to do and doing what you have to do.

One of the most practical ways that you can achieve balance is by modifying the expectations that you place on yourself. Unless you have a cape or can be in two places at the same time, you'll have to recognize and embrace your limitations.

Imagine this typical day in the life of a working mom:

The December snow is falling softly as you're driving to work, sipping on your hot cup of java. You take a deep breath, marveling at how well the last few mornings have gone. You've set a personal family record by getting out of the house on time three mornings in a row!

You get to the office, take off your coat, take a seat and turn on your computer. You've got mail. Mandatory business meeting. Ten A.M. tomorrow. You nearly choke on your coffee as you process what this means. You are supposed to be at your daughter's much-anticipated third-grade art show at that very time tomorrow—to "ooh" and "ahh" over her watercolor portrait of the family, no less. The all-too-familiar feelings of defeat and guilt begin to set in. You have to let someone down. Again.

You swallow hard. Mandatory means mandatory. There's no way out of this meeting if you want to keep your job. Your feelings are your feelings. And your daughter's feelings matter as well.

What's a working mother to do? I advise: Think creatively. Here are a few outside-the-box ideas you could try.

1. First, double-check to make sure there's not a creative alternative you can work out with your boss that would allow you to go to your daughter's art show. Could someone take notes or record the meeting for you? It never hurts to float a question by your boss, as long as she knows that you'll do all you can to work with her. (And as long as you don't take advantage of her goodwill.)

2. You could shoot an email to the art teacher explaining your situation and request a "prescreening" of the show before school. Send a camera with your daughter so that she can snap pictures during the showing and then plan a dinner date that evening to go over the pictures and talk about the day.

3. You could call on your husband, your mom or your child's favorite relative (or a friend who is like family!) to see if one of them might be willing to attend the art show with your child in your stead. Most grandmas, aunts and uncles will jump at the chance to help you out, and to spend a little quality time with your daughter in her school setting.

4. If your daughter is still disappointed, acknowledge that you understand because you are disappointed, too. Remind her that life is seldom perfect, but that you are doing your best to provide wonderful times for her in an imperfect world.

When you identify your limitations and tweak your personal expectations, you can work within your limitations. You'll learn to come up with creative ways to show that you care, even when you can't be there in person. Tend to your child's feelings, even if you can't always do everything she would like you to do. Let your child be heard and then let her know (or work with her to create) the new revised plan. Lean on your support team as you teach your child the fine art of compromise—because life is full of them! You'll come to learn that, in the end, everyone will be okay.

## Forget About the Joneses

Each family is as unique as a fingerprint—no two are the same. Resist the tendency to compare your family to others you know.

Instead, focus on your unique bunch and enjoy who you are as a team, even if you're a little unconventional.

Then help your kids focus on what you *can* do, rather than on what you can't do for them, by accentuating the positive. Although you may not be able to serve on the PTA board or share carpooling duties, find other ways to get involved that work for you and your family (and your schedule). Donating supplies, making phone calls and formatting the classroom newsletter are ways you can contribute at times that are convenient for you. Or set aside one day per year to go on a field trip with your child (if this is important to him), and plan for that day off well in advance. When you can't do the spontaneous things that pop up, you can tell your child, "I can't have lunch with you at school tomorrow, but hey, I get to go with you on the class trip to the zoo next month! Let's talk about how much fun that will be!"

## Spousal Support

Working spouses that truly tag-team parenting responsibilities are most likely to have households that run smoothly. When each spouse pitches in to help with the childcare and household management, the work and family balancing act becomes more doable. In fact, it is so important to have a supportive spouse that you need to make sure that your husband is fully behind your decision to work. Because while you may be helping to carry the family's financial load, your working *will* mean some sacrifices for him as well.

One mom I know works two evenings a week, and these have become "Dad Nights" with the kids. It's actually brought the children closer to their father, and they look forward to spending time with him and having his undivided attention. Another girlfriend of mine gets up early (4:00 A.M.!) to work as a barista while her husband tends to the morning routine of getting the kids fed and out the door to school. She gets home in time to take a nap before picking up the kids from school. Then she lets her husband rest in the evenings while she tends to the kids' baths and homework. And she and her husband still get to enjoy an hour or two of alone time after the kids are tucked away for the night.

In my last position, I worked for a family in which the mom and dad did a split shift. When I arrived for a 7 A.M. start, I was greeted by the dad, with toddlers in tow, who left for work when I arrived. At the end of the day, I did the hand-off to Mom, while Dad arrived a few hours after. Both were able to get a full day of work in, have time with the kids and even have a few minutes of family time each night. I got happy kids all day who thrived from being in a well-balanced family that modeled amazing spousal support. It certainly takes some forethought, creative planning and teamwork, but you *can* have dual incomes and a great family life.

Some moms are able to put together a "cafeteria style" childcare system that works for them and their child. For example, Tina works Tuesdays, Thursdays and Fridays from 9:30 to 3:00. She watches her neighbor's preschooler on Mondays and then her friend takes care of her four-year-old on Tuesdays (the two kids are friends, so they love their "playdate" days!). She uses a Mother's Day Out program at her local church as fun, affordable childcare while she works on Thursdays (one advantage to Mother's Day Outs is that the childcare workers aren't overtired or stressed because it is a part-time job for them). Then Grandma pitches in on Fridays. So Tina's child gets to play in a variety of places, spend time with a friend, bond with Grandma—and nobody gets overtaxed or bored.

Bottom line: Think outside the childcare box! You may be surprised what a little creativity might open up for you and your little one that could prove to be a win-win for all.

## Standing by Your Choice

I am always surprised when I hear people put down working mothers. When parents I meet in the park find out I'm a nanny, I get an earful of the opinions that they seem over-eager to share.

After I am cornered into listening to their intense (and often negative) opinions about working mothers, I often find myself asking them, "Have you ever thought about the benefits that working brings to some mothers?" I ask if they realize that if a mother is not happy with herself, she won't be happy with anyone or anything else. I ask if they have ever considered that, quite possibly, the mother is the family breadwinner, bringing home "the bacon" and providing health insurance and other necessities for the family. Then I inform them that the mother of my charges has spent the last 15 years establishing herself in her profession as an expert and if she were to step off her career track, there would be no getting back on.

I always remind them that a happy, healthy mother is an asset to her family. But if you're reading this book, you probably already know that.

Once you've decided to return to work, it's often difficult to keep yourself convinced you've made the right choice. Stay focused on the reasons why you decided to be a working mom, and don't attempt to win over the naysayers. Why? You don't have to.

If you know that you've made the right long-term choice for you and yours, that's what really matters. Turn deaf ears to those who disagree. Don't offer long-winded explanations when other people ask why you work. A simple "It is the right choice for our family" should suffice . . . and if it doesn't, save your breath. Again, embrace your choice wholeheartedly, and once you do so, others will too.

Don't be fooled into the argument of a one-size-fits-all solution for this complicated dilemma. Each mother has her own set of needs and goals that must be met for her to be the best mother she can be. If you have identified yours and are working toward reaching them, then you have no reason to buy into the working-mother guilt syndrome.

When a child has a tantrum, my advice to parents is to ignore it and not feed into the behavior. The same goes with those who look down on working mothers. You are no more and no less a mother than those who decide to stay home with their children. Let any less-than-supportive comments roll off like the proverbial water off a duck's back. Then calmly say, "I work, yes. But I'm still a full-time mother. Do you stop being a mother when you take an evening off? Or do you turn in your 'mom badge' when you go on a Mother's Day Out? There's no such thing as a part-time mother. Only full-time moms with jobs."

Remember, you've examined all the options and have decided that you are a better mother because you work, at least part-time, outside of the home. So relax. You've made a good decision! The rest of this book is dedicated to you, your family, and to making sure you feel fully supported and encouraged.

## SCENE 1: TAKE 2
### Baby's Dedication

**Aunt Claire** (*to Aunt Missy, in an irritated tone*): Can you believe she's going back to work? Why have kids if you are going to have someone else take care of them?

**Aunt Missy:** That's kind of a harsh thing to say, don't you think? It's tough for young parents to make it on one income these days.

**Aunt Claire** (*snippily*): Oh, don't even go there. She *wants* to work.

**Aunt Missy:** Whoa. You are making it sound like her decision to work means she is a bad mother. You know, besides the fact that their family may actually need the extra income, she may want to use that degree she worked four years to earn! She may find meaning in her career that helps her be a better mother. I know I was a lot happier at home when I got out of the house and worked part-time.

**Aunt Claire:** You know, you've got a point. We also lived next door to our mother and across the street from Grandma. And back then, women got together for social occasions like quilting and shelling peas. We didn't suffer from the kind of isolation women encounter these days—not having childcare and financial help from family members who live nearby.

**Aunt Missy:** You're right. And our parents' generation helped younger couples get a start in life, often by donating a piece of the family farm to them and helping them to establish their household.

**Aunt Claire:** I'm sorry. I shouldn't have been critical when I don't even know the whole situation. Her choice may be just the right one for her and her family. It's a new generation with a new way of raising families, but I know that doesn't mean it is a worse way. Just different!

**Aunt Missy** (*smiles and hugs Aunt Claire*). Now, that's the compassionate sister I know and love!

---

## HOW DID AUNT MISSY TURN THIS CONVERSATION AROUND?

- *She realized that choosing to work is a personal family decision.* There is no one-size-fits-all solution to the work-home debate.

- *She realized that making the choice to work outside of the home is difficult but often for the best.* Some women are better mothers precisely because they work outside of the home, and a working mother is no less a mother than a stay-at-home mom.

- *She showed compassion.* Family members can and should be supportive of each other's decisions.

- *She pointed out that her sister had made a harsh judgment without having all the facts.* Instead of arguing with a judgmental attitude, another's rush to judgment can be seen as an opportunity to educate.

- *She realized the importance of a career.* Investments are made to reach a high level in a career, and it is possible for a working woman to be a good mother *and* continue the good work she does out in the world.

*Q:* My parents really believe that a mother's place is in the home. How can I get them to understand that staying home full time just isn't an option for us?

**A:** In my years of experience, I have witnessed many working moms encounter surprisingly strong opposition from their parents when it comes to their decision to work or stay home. One mom put it best: "My mom truly loves us and really wants what's best. But the hard truth for her to swallow is that she doesn't really know what's best for me and my family, and though I can listen to her, the decision is not hers to make." Sometimes letting your parents know that you appreciate their love and concern can be enough to curb the unsolicited advice, but when it's not, reassure them that you've heard their opinions, and that you are going to try things differently. Promise them that if you have questions or need their input, you won't hesitate to ask them. Also, providing your parents with more information can be helpful—sharing this book or a few articles about children of working mothers can ease their worries.

**Q:** *I am a full-time working mother of a happy nine-month-old. He receives great care from my mom while I am at work, and when we are at home I spend as much time as possible with him. I even save all the household chores for after he is asleep. Why do I still feel so guilty for leaving him?*

**A:** It sounds to me like you really don't have anything to feel guilty about. The reality may be that you just miss your child. Sometimes we can be too hard on ourselves for not doing more—guilt comes from what we *aren't* doing when we gloss over what we *are* doing. Take inventory of all your accomplishments. You're fostering an awesome relationship between grandparent and grandchild; you have made it a priority to put your child first; and you are managing your career, home and motherhood. Give yourself a pat on the back and enjoy the daily time that you spend with your child.

**Q:** *I've been a stay-at-home mom for the past five years with our first child. Now that our second child is on the way, I am terribly anxious and overwhelmed with guilt because I will need to return to work shortly after her birth. How can I deal with these feelings?*

**A:** First, take a deep breath. Transitioning to the working world for any mom can be a challenge. Having a solid support system, childcare that you are confident in and a concrete plan of action for managing the logistics of day-to-day life can all help ease your anxiety. Second, remember that like each pregnancy, each child is a unique individual. Children will adapt to the environment that they are in. Instead of comparing this parenting experience with that of your older child, appreciate that this part of your parenting journey is as special and as unique as the child herself.

*Q: When I come home from a long day of work, it feels like it takes me forever to adjust to being home. I just can't figure out how to switch gears. Any ideas on how to make a smooth transition from work to home?*

**A:** One way to help you switch gears is to immediately get into your "play clothes" when you return from work. After briefly greeting your kids, work it out with your caregiver or spouse to allow you a few minutes to change and get comfortable. If you are picking up your kids from daycare and returning home as the solo adult in charge, an appropriate TV show or DVD can give everyone the few minutes they need to transition to being home. Make it a policy to avoid doing household tasks like checking email, opening the mail and returning phone calls until after the kids go to bed. This will help to keep you in mommy-mode and limit work-related distractions.

*Q: Working motherhood is really taking a toll on my relationship with my husband. At the end of the day, I am exhausted, and after the baby is asleep, the last thing I want to do is have a meaningful conversation or be intimate with my spouse. I just want to sleep. How can I keep connected to my spouse when I am always totally wiped out?*

**A:** Having a monthly date night is key to keeping connected. Schedule a time when Grandma is available to babysit and take time for just the two of you. Scheduling a call during your mutual lunch breaks, sticking Post-It love notes in your spouse's briefcase and waking up a few minutes before your child does to share morning "coffee time" with your spouse are all ways to meaningfully connect throughout the week. Also, putting your kids to bed at an appropriate time can give you more grown-up time. Even through elementary school, 8 or 8:30 is not too early to put the kids to bed. You might give older kids an hour of "quiet time" in their rooms to read or play quietly before lights out, and this, too, will give you and your husband much-needed time together.

*Q: I really love my work. I spent years getting my education and working my way up the corporate ladder. How do I respond to those who are appalled that I work because I want to, not because I have to?*

**A:** This one is easy: You don't have to respond to them. Our culture hasn't fully embraced the idea that women can work because they want to, not just because they have to. Unfortunately, the truth is that, no matter how you respond, you probably won't change the viewpoint of those who oppose you on this touchy issue. So save your breath and smile, confident that you're doing what's right for you and your family.

*Q: How can I get my husband to pitch in more around the house? I just don't think that he realizes that working all day and caring for our infant daughter all evening is taking an incredible physical and emotional toll on me. And then to have to pick up after my husband at the end of a long day—that's putting me over the edge. Help!*

**A:** Ask your husband if you can set time aside to talk about something that's been bothering you. This is a much more effective approach than venting your aggravation with him after you've just picked up his dirty socks. Be open and honest with him about your feelings, and share with him a realistic set of expectations. Ask him how you can make it easier for him to pitch in. Will leaving him a checklist of daily tasks that need to get done motivate him? Will placing the hamper in a better location help with his aim? Suggest the possibility of hiring someone to come once a week to clean the house. Figure out what he needs to make helping out a bit easier and then try to incorporate his ideas into your household management plan.

# MATERNITY LEAVE 101

SCENE 2: TAKE 1
## At the Corner Café

**Alexis** (*to Deirdre*): So, when are you going to let the cat out of the bag? You're beginning to show, you know, and the people in accounting are going to start talking.

**Deirdre** (*looking around nervously*): Quiet! You promised you wouldn't mention it while we were at work!

**Alexis** (*giggling*): Come on, you can't hide it much longer. And we're not at work—we're at lunch. So fill me in. What's your plan?

**Deirdre**: I don't have a plan! I'm not sure what to do. I want to come back after the baby arrives, but who knows if they'll even take me back? Especially since the baby is due smack dab in the middle of tax season.

**Alexis**: Oh, Deirdre, You know they need you. You're a proven asset. You've been around longer than John—and isn't he the one you'll need to talk to?

**Deirdre**: Don't remind me. I have an appointment with him next week. I have no clue what I'm going to say, but I guess I'll figure it out soon.

You just found out you're pregnant, and you're dying to announce it loudly and proudly to everyone you see. But for your own good, when it comes to the workplace, opening the employee handbook should come before opening your mouth.

The U.S. Equal Employment Opportunity Commission reports that in 2006 alone 4,901 charges of pregnancy discrimination were filed—an increase of 23 percent since 1997.[1] When compared to the same time frame, sexual harassment charges declined 32 percent, which makes the rise in pregnancy discrimination claims even more astounding.[2]

## The Legalese

First things first: What is pregnancy discrimination and how can you protect yourself from it?

"The Pregnancy Discrimination Act is an amendment to Title VII of the Civil Rights Act of 1964. Discrimination on the basis of pregnancy, childbirth or related medical conditions constitutes unlawful sex discrimination under Title VII. Women affected by pregnancy or related conditions must be treated in the same manner as other applicants or employees with similar abilities or limitations."[3] In simple terms, employers with 15 or more workers[4] cannot fire (or refuse to hire) because of pregnancy. Under this law, pregnant women are allowed to work as long as they can perform their duties and, once on maternity leave, their jobs must be held open for them. If you feel you are being discriminated against because of your pregnancy, you can file a claim through your employer or contact your local Equal Employment Opportunity Commission office (visit www.eeoc.gov to find your local office).

In addition to the Pregnancy Discrimination Act, the Family and Medical Leave Act (FMLA) may offer you additional rights.

FMLA requires companies with more than 50 people in a 75-mile radius (and all government employers) to provide up to 12 weeks of unpaid leave during any 12-month period to eligible employees (those who have worked 1,250 hours in a 12-month period) for the birth and care of a newborn, for placement with a foster or adoptive child(ren), or to care for oneself or an immediate family member with a serious health condition.[5] Men are also eligible for unpaid leave under FMLA. However, if you and your spouse work for the same company, you are limited to a combined 12 weeks of leave. You also may not qualify under FMLA if you are in the top 10 percent of earners in your company or if keeping your position open will cause the company significant financial loss.

Although it varies from state to state, you may even be eligible for paid maternity leave. In many states, such as California, New Jersey and New York for example, FMLA laws have been expanded and provide longer time off and/or paid maternity leave through the state temporary disability insurance programs.[6] In some states, the number of eligible workers a company must employ is even reduced, allowing women who work for smaller companies to receive benefits under the law.

Many employers also provide Short Term Disability (STD) insurance as part of their employee benefits package. STD pays a percentage of your salary if you become temporarily disabled and unable to work due to sickness, pregnancy or injury. "A typical STD policy provides you with a weekly portion of your salary, usually 50, 60, or 66 $2/3$ percent for 13 to 26 weeks [although 6 weeks seems to be the standard for pregnancy]."[7] If your employer does not offer STD, or if you want additional coverage, you can purchase an individual policy directly through an insurance company or agent.

With the recent growth of federal and state protection for moms-to-be, many employers already have a maternity policy in place. Check with your human resources (HR) representative or in your employee handbook for company-specific policies. Some companies restrict the order in which you can take different types of leave, although family-friendly employers sometimes allow their employees to combine sick and vacation days (and other accrued time off) during their pregnancy and maternity leave so that they can have uninterrupted income. Many women use a combination of sick time, vacation time, short-term disability, personal days and unpaid sick leave under FMLA during their time away from work.

If your employer does not have a maternity-leave policy, speak with your HR department about the development of one. Research the policies of similar types of companies, and make notes about their key features. Develop a list of common features and be sure to include them in your maternity-leave plan, citing them as industry standards.

## Planning for Maternity Leave

Now that we've covered the legal aspect of maternity leave, let's look at what it means for you. You're dying to let the cat out of the bag, but when is really the best time to break the news? Many expectant moms wait until they are into their third month, when they have confidence that their pregnancy is on track and developing normally, before they share the news with their employer.

Although FMLA laws require you to provide only 30 days notice (unless an abrupt medical condition such as pre-term labor prevents you from doing so) to be eligible for benefits (you can take your leave any time during your pregnancy or during the 12 months after the initiation of your benefits), you probably want to tell your employer before you are obviously showing—or before you tell others in the office. Officially, you want your boss to be the first to know.

When you're comfortable, you should tell your boss as professionally and unapologetically as possible that you are expecting. "I'm pleased to announce that I am expecting a baby in [insert month]" works perfectly. Avoid sharing personal details ("We've been trying for years and finally got pregnant!") and getting overly emotional ("I'm going to be a mommy!"). Short and sweet is surely the way to go when sharing the news with your boss.

Soon after you share your news, your employer will probably want to set up a meeting to talk with you about your maternity plans. But before you can negotiate your maternity plan with your boss, you need to negotiate it with yourself. Will you start your leave before you deliver or will you wait until the birth? When do you feel comfortable stopping work? How much time are you comfortable taking off? How do your finances stack up? Will your husband be taking any time off?

The birth of a baby can bring on unexpected events, feelings and emotions. Having a plan of action in your negotiating arsenal will prove beneficial to helping you secure what you want. By your third month, you should begin to develop your pregnancy and post-pregnancy plan. With complicated pregnancies or multiples, it's important to realize that the risk for unexpected bed rest increases, leaving you less time than expected to prepare for your maternity leave. Moms-to-be of twins have been known to stop work as early as at 16 weeks! If you're experiencing a complicated or a multiple pregnancy, be sure to get a head start on your planning.

Thinking through your maternity leave and your return-to-work plan before you meet with your boss will put you in a stronger negotiating position. You may also want to talk confidentially with a trusted colleague who has navigated these waters before to see how she and the company handled her leave. She may be able to provide you with insight and tips that give you a negotiating edge.

If all of this makes your head swim, read on to discover how to create your perfect pregnancy plan, step by step.

## Prepare Your Perfect Plan

Once you've familiarized yourself with the federal and state laws related to pregnancy discrimination and family leave, reviewed your company's pregnancy and maternity policies, and decided how much time you'd like (or can afford) to take off, make an outline of your ideal maternity leave "plan of action."

Your plan should be a formal proposal that includes:

- the date you intend to start your leave
- the length of your leave
- how you plan to take your leave (including the types of leave and the order you'll be taking them)
- the date you anticipate returning to work
- a list of responsibilities that will be affected because of your leave (and suggestions for how they could be handled during your absence)
- an overview of how you'd like to communicate with the office during your time away

Your proposal should also encompass your plans for returning to work. Maybe you plan on coming back part time for the first few weeks, or you would like to work a four-day week for the first six months of your return (and plan to use FMLA unpaid leave time to accomplish it)—now is the time to present your request. A professional presentation will show your employer that you've thought through your plans thoroughly and are committed to returning to work after the baby arrives.

Now is also the time to secure any upcoming reviews or evaluations. If your annual review is due to fall during your leave time, be sure to schedule it prior to your departure.

## Meet with Your Boss

Once you have outlined your ideal plan, make an appointment to meet with your human resources representative. Confirm your

## Maternity Plan Musts
www.workoptions.com/maternityleave.htm

If you've been wondering how you're going to devise your maternity plan and share it with your boss, don't worry—Pat Katepoo from WorkOptions.com has you covered. Visit her site (see the Web address above), and you'll find her free— yes, *free*—cut-paste-print Max Maternity Leave plan proposal that addresses almost everything—from planning your exit strategy to the best language to use as you negotiate the amount of leave time your emotions (and budget) can handle. The neatest thing is that she addresses many options you may not have thought of, from negotiating a job share to having a local college student do an internship to pick up the slack while you're gone! You simply cut and paste what applies to you, and voilà! A customized and professional printout is ready to present to your boss.

So what are Pat's top tips for preparing for maternity leave?

1. Do your research early. Plan ahead and become familiar with the laws that affect you as a pregnant employee.

2. Know what your company offers and what entitlements you're eligible for. What types of paid time off (PTO) does your company offer and can they be applied to your maternity leave?

3. Explore your options beyond what's in the fine print. If you have an idea, such as using your banked personal days toward your maternity leave, ask if that is an option.

4. Be proactive. Ask for what you want in your Max Maternity Leave proposal.

5. Be strategic. Develop a solid work coverage plan for when you're away. The more details you cover, the more likely you'll be able to extend your leave as your budget allows.

understanding of federal and state laws as well as company-specific policies and benefits. When you are sure that you have a thorough and complete understanding of what you can expect, schedule a time to meet with your boss.

Prepare for your meeting by reviewing your performance evaluations, promotions and contributions to the company. Identify what makes you valuable to your company, and back it up with concrete examples of your contributions. If you are responsible for managing and retaining a client base, cite the new clients that you've brought in since your employment and how your base has grown. If you handle scheduling and payroll, cite ways in which you've saved the company money. Emphasize your strengths and your areas of expertise. Highlight what sets you apart. Your goal will be to demonstrate that your skills and experience make you a valuable employee.

When you meet with your boss, be confident and professional, not emotional—remember, it's all about marketing. You are there to sell your plan to your boss. Focus on how your retention will prove financially valuable to your employer. Be sure to emphasize that you want to return to work (and how and when you plan to do so) after the birth of your child. Then suggest a specific plan that details how your workload will be divided during your absence and how you will transition back upon your return.

A written overview of your duties and responsibilities and a map of your office (and desk!) will be extremely valuable to your colleagues while you are away. Be sure to bring a copy home with you so that if you are contacted by a lost and searching soul looking for a client file whose whereabouts are known only to you, you'll be able to help that person out. Creating a flowchart with major deadlines, developing a contact list for current vendors and clients, organizing your office (or making detailed notes about your "unique" filing system), writing out your day-to-day required tasks, and providing valuable and time-sensitive information to those who will be covering for you while you are gone will all be greatly appreciated, and will show your employer and coworkers your loyalty, dedication and commitment to teamwork and company success.

Try to anticipate some of the questions that may cross your boss's mind as you discuss your proposal, and be ready to respond. Who will oversee project deadlines? Who will manage your responsibilities? Who will take over your day-to-day tasks? Are you sure you are coming back? Will you be accessible during your leave (by email, fax and phone)? These are just some of the common questions employers struggle with when faced with an expectant mom's request for extended leave.

Most of all, during this process you also need to be prepared to compromise. Tack on an additional two weeks to your leave proposal so that you have room to negotiate with respect to the length of time you want to take off. If you plan on returning part time, be prepared to take a pay cut or devise a plan to reduce your workload. If you want to work from home one day a week, offer to come back to the office a bit sooner and stretch out your leave by taking a day off each week during your first few months back.

You also need to think through the possible arguments your boss will have concerning your plan and formulate winning responses in your mind, ahead of time. If you plan to telecommute, be prepared to share the benefits your boss will reap, such as your uninterrupted work time, no commute, saved office space, extended hours resulting in increased productivity. If your leave extends through a major annual company deadline, suggest doing project-specific work from home so that you can still deliver the goods. If your boss seems to be wavering on accepting your plan, suggest a trial period.

In most cases, an employer will rarely turn down a well-thought-out and detailed leave plan, because when presented professionally, your boss will likely see that it is cheaper to keep you than to find, hire and train someone new.

If you are met with resistance, be ready to evaluate whether or not this company will be family-friendly enough for you to continue with once you have a family of your own. There are a growing number of businesses that pride themselves on their support of families by offering generous flex-time arrangements for working parents. These companies even recruit mothers who have left the workforce temporarily to raise their kids because they see in these women the value of their education, training, skills and experience.

Want to know if your company makes the cut? Each year *Working Mother Magazine* releases its list of the 100 best companies for working moms. To make the list, companies are judged on five criteria: flexibility, leave for new parents, childcare, elder care and the number of women occupying top company positions. Check out www.workingmother.com to view this year's top picks.

## Begin Your Professional Pregnancy Pause

So you've developed your plan, you've worked out the details with your boss and you're satisfied with the outcome. It's now time to enter into your professional pregnancy pause. Pack up your personal office mementos, keep things professional, keep the lines of communication open, and be sure to have a plan in place so that you can notify your company when your new bundle of joy arrives.

SCENE 2: TAKE 2
*At the Corner Café*

**Alexis** *(to Deirdre):* So, when are you going to let the cat out of the bag? You're beginning to show you know, and the people in accounting are going to start talking.

**Deirdre** *(looking around nervously):* Quiet! You promised you wouldn't mention it while we were at work! I haven't officially made the announcement to John.

**Alexis** *(giggling):* Come on, you can't hide it much longer. And we're not at work—we're at lunch. So fill me in. What's your plan?

**Deirdre** *(excited):* I'm working on it. I can't believe how much information is out there on maternity leave benefits and rights. Do you know they can't let me go because I'm pregnant—or make me come back before I'm ready? They may be stuck with me!

**Alexis:** Oh, Deirdre, they're hardly stuck with you! They need you. You're a proven asset. You've been around longer than John—and isn't he the one you'll need to talk to?

**Deirdre:** Yes, and you're right! I've looked over my personal records and my performance evaluations. The company does need me. I have an appointment with John next week. I'm putting together a detailed plan for both my leave and my reentry. I really feel good about it, now that I know my rights and where I stand.

**Alexis:** Good for you! John knows you're the detail queen, so I'm sure he won't be surprised.

---

## WHY WAS DEIRDRE CONFIDENT ABOUT REQUESTING HER MATERNITY LEAVE?

- *She had kept her pregnancy low key until she told her boss.* Understand the value of hearing the news from the horse's mouth, rather than through the grapevine.

- *She knew her rights.* Do your research and discover what your rights and benefits are under the law.

- *She knew her value.* Look over your past personnel evaluations and performance reviews so that you can be specific about your contributions.

- *She put together a plan.* Have a well-thought-out pregnancy leave and reentry plan that you can present to your employer.

- *She had a proven track record.* Your reputation for attention to detail and overall competence will carry over to your proposal.

 & A

**Q:** *I'm still in my first trimester and don't want to tell anyone at work that I am expecting yet. My problem is that because I am having a high-risk pregnancy, I have weekly doctor appointments that I can't miss. What can I do?*

**A:** When you decide to share the news of your pregnancy with others really is a personal choice, so you need not feel bad about keeping it a secret. Many doctors offer early morning or evening appointments to accommodate working moms-to-be. Others will allow you to book out appointment times weeks in advance so that you can choose times that work well for you, such as during your lunch break or the first or last appointment of the day. If your appointment must fall during your working day, the best thing you can do is speak with your boss. Explain that you are having some personal medical issues that require you to keep a weekly doctor appointment and that you will adjust your hours to make up for the time that you are out of the office.

*Q:* *I am really excited to be expecting, but I am also really nervous that I may lose my job due to my pregnancy. I need to work. How can I be sure my position is secure?*

**A:** First, determine if your position is covered under the Pregnancy Discrimination Act (PDA). The PDA is a federal law that prohibits discrimination against pregnant workers. It also states that employers must hold a job open for a pregnancy-related absence for the same length of time positions are held for those who are sick or on disability leave. The Family and Medical Leave Act (FMLA) also provides protection for eligible employees, allowing them to take up to 12 weeks of unpaid leave to care for a newborn or adopted child. However, if you work for a company that has fewer than 15 employees, your position may not be protected. Your best bet is to contact the Equal Employment Opportunity Commission (EEOC) and to make an appointment with your human resources representative to better understand your rights and your employer's maternity leave policy.

*Q:* *I asked my husband to inquire about taking a paternity leave. He looked at me like I had three heads and said he's never heard of such a thing. Is paternity leave a standard benefit most employers offer?*

**A:** Although most new dads take time off as vacation time or sick time, many are now opting to take unpaid leave under the Family and Medical Leave Act (FMLA). If your husband has worked for a company with more than 50 employees for the past 12 months or if he is a federal or state employee, he is likely eligible to take time off under the FMLA. But if your husband is in the top 10 percent of wage earners or if his absence will cause substantial economic harm to his company, he may not be eligible. Best bet: Have him make an appointment with his human resources department and research together your state laws regarding paternity leave and FMLA. Sometimes those who aren't eligible under FMLA may still be eligible for time off under their state laws, which are often more generous than FMLA.

*Q: I am planning on returning to work after the birth of my child, but I am afraid once the baby is here, my feelings may change. How can I be sure I am making the right decision to return to work?*

**A:** It's great that you have an honest outlook and understand that your feelings may change. And it's okay if they do! One working mom-to-be, who was afraid that her hormones were dictating her decision rather than her brain, decided to plan for as much maternity leave time as possible. She recently shared, "The added time I took off allowed me to adjust to motherhood and to evaluate in the here and now based on my current feelings, rather than feeling forced to make a speculative decision so far in advance." She now advises other moms-to-be in her workplace to "pig pile their vacation time, sick time and non-paid leave to allow themselves the time that they need to make a decision that is right for them once the baby has arrived."

*Q: I am expecting my third child, and even though I've remained at the same place of employment during all my pregnancy and births, my boss keeps teasing me, saying that "This time I know you won't come back." It is really frustrating! How can I get him to stop?*

**A:** I agree; that *is* frustrating. Fortunately you are protected from unwanted verbal comments or jokes about your pregnancy under the Pregnancy Discrimination Act, so you're well within your rights to speak up. Chances are, because you've been at your place of employment so long, you probably have a decent enough relationship with your boss to pull him aside and let him know that his comments are bothering you. The next time he makes one of his jokes, pull him aside and say something like, "I know you probably mean no harm, but the truth is the continual comments about my returning to work are really bothering me. Please stop." If this doesn't nip it in the bud, follow up with a written complaint to his supervisor and/or the EEOC.

*Q: I'm expecting my first child, but I am not married. Am I still protected under the same laws as married pregnant women?*

**A:** Although the Equal Employment Opportunity Commission does not discriminate based on marital status, some state and local laws may. To better understand your rights, you'll need to research your state and local laws. A good place to start is your state government's website.

*Q: I work in an environment that exposes me to harsh chemicals and heavy lifting. How can I be sure that my baby is safe while I am at work?*

**A:** By law, your employer must accommodate your pregnancy, as it is legally considered a temporary disability. For a job that involves heavy lifting or strenuous work, your employer may be required to provide a light-duty work assignment for you. However, you'll need to do some research as the laws vary from state to state. The Occupational Safety and Health Administration (OSHA) and the Organization of Teratology Information Services (OTIS) are great resources for helping you and your employer determine what is safe for you during your pregnancy.

# EXHAUSTION, CRAVINGS, CRYING, NAUSEA AND NESTING ON THE JOB

## SCENE 3: TAKE 1
### *At a Second-Trimester Checkup*

**Dr. Stands** (*to Grace*): Hi, Mrs. Renten, how are you feeling?

**Grace** (*eyes welling up with tears*): I'm feeling tired, nauseous and fat. Very fat.

**Dr. Stands** (*chuckling*): Well, it sounds like everything is progressing normally.

**Grace:** Everyone keeps telling me I'll feel better soon, but it doesn't help when I'm falling asleep at my desk and constantly on the hunt for food. My staff keeps bringing me bags of peanut M&Ms to calm my "hungries." At least it's a change from the first trimester when I couldn't keep anything down and was always racing for the bathroom or searching frantically for the wastebasket.

**Dr. Stands:** Well, your body is certainly going through many changes right now. Rest assured that what you're experiencing is normal, but it's really important to take it easy when you're feeling tired, eat when you're hungry and begin to think about how you'll cut back on your workload.

**Grace**: Take it easy? Cut back? I can't!

Managing the hormonal and physical discomforts of pregnancy for working moms-to-be quickly becomes a part-time job in and of itself. Unlike a race car, that goes from 0 to 60 in a matter of seconds, your body takes its own sweet time as it goes through the complex—but wonderfully miraculous—process of shifting gears as it grows one miniscule fertilized cell into an eightish-pound bundle of joy.

Even the most normal of pregnancies will have its share of physical discomforts and emotional upsets, and if you're carrying twins (or more!), the multiple blessings often bring multiplied discomfort. So how can you possibly manage all the changes that your body is undergoing to prepare you for mommyhood, while spending your days under the watchful eyes of your boss and coworkers?

## The Fatigue Factor

In the early weeks, and again in the final weeks, of pregnancy, fatigue is often your biggest enemy. You knew the time would come when you could no longer manage your normal workload, but you never knew that time would come so soon. Jeanie, a project manager, was surprised that her toughest days were the early days: "I had so much work to tie up before I started feeling *really* bad and *really* pregnant, but I was simply amazed at how little energy I had and how much more sleep I seemed to require for being so newly pregnant."

When you are working outside of the home (and even more so if you are working outside of the home *and* chasing a toddler or two), it's imperative that you understand that your ever-growing body needs rest—and lots of it. So what can you do to fight off the fatigue?

Be sure to get a solid eight hours of sleep. When worries or fears overwhelm you at night (or vivid dreams of all sorts flood your mind), try to unwind. Ask your husband for a gentle back rub, take a hot bath, read a book (preferably not a real page-turner) or your favorite pregnancy magazine.

Many moms-to-be also find that insomnia can be a real issue toward the end of pregnancy. Lisa swore her baby was nocturnal—sleeping all day then trying to kick out of her womb at night. The discomfort, along with frequent bathroom trips and vivid dreams, kept her from getting more than an hour or two of shut-eye at a time. She found that taking a warm shower and then positioning herself in bed with tons of pillows provided some relief. Other mothers take a book to bed, along with a warm cup of milk to help pave the way to la-la land. *Chicken Soup for the Expectant Mother's Soul* is a great book filled with stories short enough for overtired eyes to get through but long enough to help you relax and get ready for a good long snooze. Closing your eyes and slowly relaxing each part of your body from head to toe is also a wonderful way to relax into dreamland.

During the day at work, find time to rest, especially if you're having a hard time sleeping at night. Talking yourself into resting briefly during the day (and not feeling guilty about doing it) is a skill you need to master. Ideally, try to lie down for a few minutes if there is a couch in the lounge or women's area. Or bring a mat, pillow and blanket, lock your office door during your break and doze on your nap pad, just like you used to do in kindergarten!

If getting prone is not feasible at your workplace, take five to seven minutes to stretch your muscles into a "rag doll" pose (tightening then loosing groups of muscles) while sitting at your desk. Drink a bottle of water and enjoy a wholesome snack. Have your mp3 player ready, loaded with your favorite easy-listening tunes. As your break time draws to a close, apply lip balm and lotion in an invigorating scent to give yourself a little pick-me-up before heading back to duty (just be sure you choose one that won't make you sick—more on that to come).

Now is also the time to begin to ask for—and accept—help with work projects when you need it. Your body is using lots of energy to support two (or more), and you're sure to be tired, drained and definitely in need of a helping hand when you're not feeling up to par. Most of your coworkers will understand, especially working moms who've "been there." And most people love to feel needed, so ask for help. Allow them to enjoy the gift of being generous. Someday you'll return the favor for another pregnant working mom.

One last word of advice: Be selective and compassionate with yourself when choosing which projects and how many of them to tackle. Less really is more right now.

## Hassling Headaches and Heartburn Galore

You may also find that as your belly grows, your head seems to be expanding as well, from the constant throbbing that's going on up there. Although headaches tend to only last until mid-pregnancy, depending on their severity, they can be temporarily debilitating, and can literally be a pain. Fatigue, dehydration (it's so hard to guzzle those eight-plus glasses, but you can do it!), low blood sugar (from skipping meals when you're rushed) and stress can contribute to major pain in your noggin.

Although it's easier said than done, relaxation can certainly help alleviate brain pain. Lying down at home with a cold compress on your head, getting a gentle back massage, drinking a warm cup of cocoa, having a nutritious snack—such as apples with peanut butter—are all great ways to ease headaches caused by tension. While at work, be sure to keep your locker or desk (and your purse) stocked with snacks (protein bars are compact and convenient) and water, and put an ice pack in the office fridge to use should a headache strike you midday.

What about pain meds? Ask your doctor. If you can handle the pain without drugs, it is probably best to use natural methods to remedy your discomfort. If the pain is blinding, then your doctor may be able to prescribe or recommend a painkiller that won't harm your growing baby.

Indigestion and heartburn are other frequent visitors to your pregnant self, especially in the last trimester. That burning sensation in the upper abdomen or lower chest (the kind that makes you think you might be having a heart attack) is often intensified during pregnancy. The hormonal changes that affect the stomach muscles and the pressure of the uterus on the stomach are the culprits of this ever-present discomfort.

Specific foods can also be indigestion triggers. Jan, a manager at a chain restaurant, said that foods she ate pre-pregnancy—and never bothered her—were a source of torture now. Avoiding certain foods is one way to avoid some episodes of heartburn. Greasy fried foods, soda, chocolate (yikes!), coffee, tea and acidic foods (such as orange juice and tomatoes) are known causes of irritation. Lying down right after eating or snacking before bedtime can also exacerbate the problem. A glass of milk or a cup of vanilla yogurt, a bowl of mild cereal or a nice serving of warm oatmeal are good late-night snack choices that generally soothe the stomach and esophagus. Doctors often allow you to eat Tums or antacids that have plenty of calcium, as they are actually good for your baby's growing bones (but again, always check with your personal physician to find out which indigestion reliever is right for you).

Eating five small, evenly spaced meals throughout the day, rather than three large ones, can help you maintain balanced sugar levels and prevent hunger-related mood swings. When you're on the job, resist the urge to get fast food, and instead try packing an insulated bag or cooler (the night before) with some fresh fruits and vegetables, whole grain bread with cheese and yogurt, and slices of meat to keep you going through the day. A jar of peanut butter (don't forget to keep a supply of plastic spoons in your desk drawer) can quickly satisfy your cravings and give you a protein boost any time.

Lora, who works in a downtown marketing firm, found that sticking to the basics on the days she had presentations and meetings helped keep her stomach in check: "On the days I had to meet with clients, I was sure to stick with bagels, skip my morning cup of coffee and avoid foods that tended to give me trouble with indigestion or heartburn."

## Ravenous Cravings

Pickles and ice cream. Potato chips and mayo. Cookie dough, straight from the fridge. Worcherstire sauce and parmesan cheese (no kidding on that last combo—one of my friends went through jars of this stuff, mixed together!). Weird concoctions are often considered more desirable than a gourmet four-course meal for many a pregnant mom-to-be.

Cravings, or the intense desire for certain foods or combinations of foods that you would not normally eat, are common among expectant moms. Actually, studies show that 75 percent of women indulge in such cravings during pregnancy, with the most common cravings being chocolate, pickles, ice cream, citrus fruits and chips.[1]

Maybe you've experienced a bizarre craving and wondered why. Some attribute cravings to the body's response to a lack of certain nutrients in the diet, and others consider them to be without rhyme or reason. Regardless, you are likely to crave strange foods and to be hungry—often—throughout your pregnancy. That is, once food stops making you nauseous (we're coming to that!).

As long as satisfying food cravings doesn't replace good nutrition for more than a day or two, there is no cause for alarm. However, if you're finding your daily diet limited to eggs and mustard, check with your doctor to make sure you are getting all the nutrients your baby needs (and don't forget how important it is to take your prenatal vitamin daily, especially in the early months). You should also call your doctor if you're faced with nonfood cravings (not unheard of during pregnancy—don't laugh) for things such as dirt or laundry starch. Anemia is a common cause of pica, or nonfood cravings.

So when you're at work and don't have access to your arsenal of food, how can you manage your midday cravings? Again, be sure to stock up. I often advise moms-to-be to keep a designated snack bag in the car and one at the office; granola bars, dried fruits, trail mix, small tins of tuna, cheese sticks, nuts and wheat crackers are great snack choices. Be sure to keep bottled water on hand as well to keep you hydrated. And yes, you can indulge your desire for chocolate, but limit the amount to a very few ounces, and for the best burst of antioxidants, the darker the chocolate the better.

## Tummy Turnings

Depending on what stage of pregnancy you're in, the mere mention of food can be enough to make you sick to your stomach. One pregnant friend couldn't tolerate the smell or taste of toothpaste and had to go with baking soda for the duration. Nausea and vomiting are two of the symptoms of early pregnancy that can make functioning—never mind working—nearly impossible.

Unlike normal non-pregnancy nausea that screams loud and clear "Don't eat!" nausea during pregnancy can actually be your body's signal for saying, "I'm overdue for some food!"

Eating small, protein-rich meals throughout the day can help stave off nausea. A good guideline to follow is to eat three small meals and two to three snacks each day, whether you feel hungry or not. Remember, your pregnant body requires around 400 additional calories a day to support your growing baby.

Beyond eating small meals several times during the day, some women find that eating a saltine cracker as soon as they wake up (before even sitting up) can help with morning sickness. Many moms-to-be also rely on Preggo Pops (lollipops sold commonly at Motherhood Maternity) to curb their nausea. Some women swear by lemons, both the smell and the taste of them. Amy carried a lemon everywhere she went, cut in half; she sniffed its fragrance and licked the juice whenever she started to feel queasy. You can also talk to your doctor about nausea-reducing medications.

In the real world, of course, staving off nausea isn't always possible. If you tend to experience morning sickness in the early morning before heading off to work, it's going to take some planning to get you to work safely. When public transportation and car pooling aren't options and you have to tackle the traffic on your own, here are a few tips to keep in mind.

- Take a cool glass of water with you, which can help fend off nausea.

- Cool air on the face can also help, so even if it's mid-winter, roll down the windows of your car as you drive to and from work and put a small fan on your desk at work.

- Become familiar with a few safe places along your driving route so that you can pull over and wait for the nausea to subside.

• Keep those bags handy—gallon-size Ziploc bags work especially well (I use them with kids who get car sick) because you can seal up the bag after you make your deposit.

On some days, you may need to freshen up a bit once you arrive at your workplace. Keep a spare work-appropriate outfit in your car, along with some facial wipes (Pond's Facial Wipes are my personal fave). A toothbrush, toothpaste and mouthwash can make the day more bearable for you—and your coworkers!

You'll also want to keep in mind the shortest route to the closest bathroom in the facility where you're working, whether you're offsite or in your own building. If you don't have a private office, enlist an office or cubicle mate to help with your quick escape. Coming up with a code word for when you are going to be sick can signal to that special someone to cover your desk while you head off to the closest stall. The downside of enlisting help is that it may make it a bit harder to keep things under wraps if you're trying to keep your pregnancy quiet in the early months—so be sure to choose a coworker you trust.

What if you're about to give a presentation and a bout of morning sickness strikes? What then? Although it may go against your natural desire for privacy, being open and honest about how you're feeling during your pregnancy is your best bet. Having a confidential chat, sooner rather than later, will prevent your coworkers and clients from forming misconceptions about the reason for your suddenly decreased energy level and frequent "breaks."

You should also be prepared to excuse yourself, professionally but promptly, if the time comes when you're about to toss your cookies while in a meeting or giving a lecture. A subtle but sharp exiting statement such as "Excuse me, I need a moment" should suffice, but if you're afraid people are going to ask questions, then "Excuse me! I'm going to be sick" will usually put any inquiries at a halt. In fact, you'll probably find the room of execs will gladly cut a wide swath to facilitate your exit.

## When the Fluids Are Flowing

During your pregnancy, you'll quickly notice (and chances are your coworkers will too) that you're making more frequent trips to the restroom. Hormonal changes and the position of your ever-growing uterus are to blame. To make the best of your new closer relationship to your office lavatory, realize that this part of pregnancy is inevitable. Regardless of how inconvenient it can be, never try to hold out till the end of a meeting or project. It's not good for your bladder, not good for the baby and it's mighty uncomfortable!

You may also be surprised to discover an increase in vaginal secretions during pregnancy (one of my friends joked, "It felt like I was holding a peanut butter sandwich between my legs for nine months!"). Again, blame the hormones. Super-absorbent cotton panties can help you cope with excess fluids. Although you'll want to stay away from sanitary pads that tend to cause irritation, think about investing in cotton panty liners (Lotus Pads makes a great washable cotton panty liner—check out www.lotuspads.com).

During this new phase of your life, you'll also want to be on the lookout for vaginal infections that are common during pregnancy. Be sure to call your healthcare provider if you have any telltale itchiness or irritation so that you can get the proper treatment as soon as possible and nip any impending infection in the bud. The new line of yogurts with extra probiotics is wonderful for preventing yeast overgrowth in your digestive system and vaginal canal. If you're into natural remedies, try eating one a day and see if it doesn't do the trick for you.

An increased production of saliva is also common during pregnancy, although this symptom tends to decrease as pregnancy progresses. No one really knows why chewing gum seems to help, but it does. Be sure to have a variety on hand while at work so that you are sure to have a flavor you can tolerate.

## Aches and Pains

Lower backaches, leg cramps and all-around aches and pains go hand in hand with pregnancy. Although you can't stop them completely, you can take some practical measures to lessen your discomfort.

Dressing comfortably for work is key. Be sure to trade in your heels for a good pair of supportive flats and your tight-waisted suit pants for a stretchy cotton alternative. You may also want to purchase a maternity belt that can be worn under your clothing to help support your lower back and growing belly.

While at work, try not to assume the same position for too long. Alternate between sitting (avoid sitting with your legs crossed) and standing when you can, and if you're feeling up to it, incorporate a small walk into your day. Propping your legs on a small stool while sitting at your desk can also relieve some of the strain caused by the chair pressure under your thighs. One working mom-to-be recently told me that she was in a meeting and had to change chairs three times before she found one that she could get comfortable in. (Her preference would have been to lie on her side on the floor, but CEOs tend to frown on their employees lying on the carpet during board meetings—go figure!)

Daily stretching can also be a source of much-needed relief. Ankle circles and calf stretches (pointing your heel instead of your toes) can be done easily under the cover of your desk. If you're feeling a bit cramped under the ribs, try stretching with your arms to the side and over your head, then alternate with individual shoulder lifts to relieve the pain.

## Tissues, Please

You may or may not be prepared for the emotional flood that accompanies even the most stress-free of pregnancies.

From worrying about whether you're going to be a good mom to sudden inexplicable mood swings to irritability, anxiety and depression, emotions run high during this time.

First, know that what you're feeling (or may not be feeling) is normal. Your emotions are simply responses to the chemical, physical and external changes that are taking place in your body and in your life. Also, know that these feelings will pass; they are temporary. Making light—when you can—of your emotional "episodes" will help. "Pass the chocolates and Kleenex," you might say, "I've got a hormonal wave coming on!" even as the tears roll down your cheeks for no particular reason. You might as well smile and be lighthearted—you'll feel better and you'll ease the discomfort of those around you.

One mom-to-be who was nervous about her upcoming delivery was surprised to learn that her husband also had concerns and fears. Sharing how you are feeling with your partner and a few close friends can be a great source of encouragement. Having a friend to listen and comfort you when you're going through the pre-baby blues can be just what you need to make you feel a bit better. A group of girlfriends I know made a pact that they'd always take any pregnant friend out to her favorite place for lunch during her ninth month. Pampering goes a long way toward easing the way in your final days before labor. That same group made a commitment to purposely pray for the pregnant lady (and we all know the prayers of a righteous group of women avail much!).

A word of caution is in order here. During this time, you may have a lot of well-meaning friends, family or coworkers sharing their advice, which is fine—but don't feel obligated to take it. Some of the most common advice has its source in old wives' tales, rather than medical facts.

While at work, keep a journal so that you always have an outlet for expressing your feelings. Yes, you may have a confidante or two at work whom you can go to if you really need to talk, and that's wonderful—but your journal is ever-present. When feelings well up, you can nearly always grab a pen to put them on paper. One of the most soothing books/journals for moms of faith is called *The Child Within* by Mary Hanes. Though it is out of print, you can buy a cheap copy utilizing Amazon's online used-book option. Or you can just type in the words "pregnancy journal" in any major bookseller's website search engine and several titles will pop up—one is bound to suit your taste and needs. Keeping a journal is a great way to chart your baby's growth (and yours), celebrate each stage of your pregnancy and joyfully anticipate your baby's birthing day! The safe haven for your feelings, your pregnancy journal will not only be a comfort to you during your wait but also a joy to you in coming years.

## Unusual Urges

You're about five months into your pregnancy and now, out of the blue, you are overcome with the intense desire to throw away all of your cooking utensils and purchase new ones. Why? You've been attacked by the nesting bug, the uncontrollable urge to clean everything—and yes, I mean everything—in order to prepare a "nest" for your soon-to-arrive bundle of joy.

Although the experiences of moms vary, the nesting impulse seems to bring about some pretty unique and seemingly irrational behaviors for most. From cleaning the bathroom floors with a toothbrush to scrubbing almost everything in the house, moms have been known to turn into Martha Stewart (with a big belly) on fast-forward in the name of providing a super clean and organized home in which to welcome their new arrival. (Either that or an intense fear of impending mothers'-in-law cleanliness inspections takes over pregnant mothers' minds, en masse.)

Nesting in itself is rarely of concern, but there are a few things to keep in mind. Stay away from the litter box and working in soil that may be contaminated with cat feces (this one is not a wives' tale). Cat feces can contain a parasite that causes toxoplasmosis, a rare but serious blood infection that can cause birth defects. I know how much you just *hate* to have to turn over the cat box cleaning duties to your hubby for nine months, but just force yourself to do so.

You'll also want to be sure to keep the areas that you are cleaning well-ventilated and to never mix ammonia with bleach cleaning products. You should also steer clear of painting projects, unless you're only using water-based products. Still, when it comes to involved, strenuous painting activities, it's a good time to delegate—you pick and choose the colors, then have someone else do the actual work.

Although nesting is a wonderful way to prepare for your new arrival, it can be problematic to have a "nesting attack" while at the office. So when you're sitting at your desk and you start thinking about your to-do list back home, get out a pen and paper and start writing down your projects to get them off your mind. If the list turns out to be more than three-feet long, save it. Tuck it into your pregnancy journal and a year or so later—when you are too tired to even think of cleaning a bathtub after rocking your baby all night—get out the list, and smile at the supermom energy you once had.

## SCENE 3: TAKE 2
### At a Second-Trimester Checkup

**Dr. Stands** (*to Grace*): Hi, Mrs. Renten, how are you feeling?

**Grace** (*welling up with tears*): I'm feeling tired, nauseous and fat. Very fat.

**Dr. Stands** (*chuckling*): Well, it seems like everything is progressing normally then.

**Grace:** I guess I didn't know normal would feel, well, this *abnormal*. Boy, is my body changing! I never dreamed I'd be this tired. Or hungry. Maybe I'm making up for the first three months when I upchucked everything I ate.

**Dr. Stands** (*smiling*): Well, your body is certainly going through many changes right now. Rest assured that what you're experiencing is normal, but it's really important to take it easy when you're feeling tired, eat when you're hungry and begin to think about how you'll cut back on your workload. Get a little "Just Say No" sign and put it where you can see it!

**Grace:** I actually have a "pregnancy assessment" meeting scheduled with my boss to talk to her about my maternity plans—and I've got a little "pamper myself" pregnancy stash of goodies in my office desk: nutritious snacks, bottled water and boxed juices, and a little napping mat with a pillow and blanket, just like I had in kindergarten. Except now I have an iPod uploaded with soothing music that calms my nerves and helps me relax. I eat lunch in my office so I can use some of my break to take a real nap.

**Dr. Stands:** That a girl! I wish you could talk to some of my pregnant working clients who don't take my advice seriously and end up ill or exhausted. If you love that baby, you've got to care for yourself as well as you can!

---

## WHAT STEPS DID GRACE TAKE TO SUCCESSFULLY HANDLE HER PREGNANCY-RELATED "CHALLENGES" WHILE ON THE JOB?

- *She was open about her feelings.* Share with your doctor how you are feeling, accept his or her support and advice, and know that what you are experiencing is normal.

- *She realized the reality of the body changes she was experiencing.* Accept that your changing body will affect your mood, your energy levels and your ability to handle your everyday workload.

- *She was proactive in self-care.* Schedule a pregnancy-assessment meeting with your boss to keep him or her informed about how you are doing with your workload. Be purposeful about setting aside break times to get the nutrition and rest that you need.

- *She had a maternity plan prepared.* Having an open conversation about your pre-birth and post-labor plans will help to eliminate confusion and guesswork for you and your boss.

---

**Q:** *I am in my second trimester and have horrible headaches! I'm not quite sure what to do—they hurt so badly that they interfere with my ability to work. Any suggestions?*

**A:** The intensity of the headaches that I experienced during the second trimester of my pregnancy was probably the most surprising symptom that I encountered. By mid-pregnancy, your body fluids have increased 40 to 60 percent, and it takes a bit of time for your body to adjust to the changes in circulation and the increased pressure on your blood vessels. I've found that drinking plenty of water, eating a well-balanced pregnancy diet, getting enough rest and limiting stress and anxiety can help curb second trimester headaches. You may also want to check out a massage therapist who specializes in prenatal massage. If they are skilled, they can be a wonderful source of nonmedical pain relief throughout your entire pregnancy, and the health benefits of massage are numerous: relaxation, increased circulation and all that extra pampering that pregnant women need!

A lesser-known resource, but one that is growing in popularity, is to hire a doula, which is a lot like hiring a nanny for yourself (see www.dona.org for more information). Doulas are informed companions who help comfort and coach women through pregnancy, childbirth and post-partum adjustment. Doulas are especially wonderful for women who live far away from their moms, sisters or close friends and need a companion/friend to help them along. Some doulas do prenatal massage, while others help with your older children so that you can be focused on your baby—basically she takes the role that your mom or best friend would take if they lived nearby!

*Q: How can I be sure that my boss knows I am still working hard, even though I've had to cut back from working 12-hour days to working 8- to 9-hour days?*

**A:** Although some employers equate long hours with hard work, it's not necessarily the case. The best way you can make the most of your time in the office is to increase the efficiency with which you work. This may mean less time returning personal phone calls or emails while on the clock and keeping office chitchat to a minimum. It also means delegating tasks to others when you can. If you feel like your pace has significantly slowed, you may want to consider coming into work early or staying late one night per week to catch up. Let your boss know that you've readjusted your schedule, keep her informed of your work progress, and keep track of your accomplishments so that you can document what you've contributed to the company during your pregnancy.

*Q: I am one of only two women in my office and the first to be pregnant. What is the best way to handle my pregnancy?*

**A:** These uncharted waters can certainly work in your favor. Because you are the first woman to be pregnant on the job, if you play your cards right, you have the opportunity to set a positive precedent. Maintaining your professionalism, presenting your requests for additional breaks or other special treatment with confidence, and continuing to work as diligently as possible increase your chances of getting exactly what you want and need. If you come up against opposition, research the policies of similar companies in your area and present your findings as the industry standard in your area.

*Q: I sit at a computer all day and it's killing me. I just can't get comfortable. What can I do?*

**A:** If possible, you may want to invest in a chair of your own or trade in your current model for a chair that you find particularly comfortable. A chair with adjustable armrests, firm seat and back cushions, together with an ottoman, can help make hours of sitting much easier. If purchasing a new chair on your own isn't possible, improvise with what you have by using a pillow for extra back support. You can also rest your feet on an upside-down wastebasket or box.

*Q: My employer is trying to talk me into taking maternity leave much earlier than I had planned. He says I am tired and need the rest. Am I obligated to take his advice?*

**A:** Pregnant employees must be permitted to work as long as they are able to perform their job-related duties. If an employee is temporarily unable to perform her job due to her pregnancy, the employer must treat her in the same way he would any other temporarily disabled employee. Under the Pregnancy Discriminatory Act (PDA), an employer can't force a pregnant woman to take time off during her pregnancy or force her to quit because of fears that the work she is doing may be hazardous to her or her unborn child (though of course you need to exercise good judgment in this area!).

*Q: My job requires a lot of air travel. With morning sickness and the other discomforts of pregnancy, I'm just not feeling up to it. Can I refuse?*

**A:** According to attorney Jack Tuckner, an expert in Pregnancy Discrimination Law, if you are having medical challenges related to your pregnancy, your employer must reasonably accommodate those challenges and provide you with suitable working alternatives. What it really comes down to is your employer providing you with the same treatment that any other temporarily disabled worker would receive. The success of your request will depend on numerous factors, such as the duration of the requested accommodation (if you can't fly for nine months it's less likely to pass muster than if you can't fly for just six weeks); the nature of your medical issues (a typical case of "morning sickness" will be treated differently from certain bona fide high-risk pregnancy conditions); the percentage of your job responsibilities that involve air travel; the size of your company; how many other employees can assume your job-related duties that involve air travel; and whether or not there are any in-office job duties that you can fulfill while you're "grounded."

If air travel is the primary essential function of your job (as is the case with pilots and flight attendants) and you are no longer able to perform the duties of your job due to a pregnancy-related condition, then you may no longer be permitted to work, since you are effectively "disabled." In that event, you would probably have to apply for short-term disability until you are again able to perform your job functions. Since laws vary from state to state (and state laws can often be more generous than federal laws), do your research and be sure to understand your rights before making any job-related decisions.

# SECTION 2

## Mixing Babies with Business

# 4

# LEAVING YOUR PRECIOUS BUNDLE IN LOVING ARMS

## SCENE 4: TAKE 1
### *On the Phone*

**Cheryl** (*to Paula*): Did I tell you Ken said I could bring Addyson to work for the first few weeks? I am so relieved.

**Paula**: No, you didn't. That's great news! You must be thrilled.

**Cheryl**: Really, it is wonderful. It buys me a little more time to decide what I want to do for the long term.

**Paula**: Yeah, you mentioned the other day that you had begun the childcare search. Any luck?

**Cheryl**: At this point I need more than luck. I'm so overwhelmed. There are just too many options, each with a set of pros and cons. I don't know what to do. I am really at a loss. This is much harder than I ever imagined.

**Paula**: Well, once you sort through your options, you'll find what's best. I'm sure of it!

You expected labor to be hard (I did—but it was still a surprise!). You knew giving birth could be a long, difficult process and that it could even bring unexpected complications. You anticipated a few sleepless nights and knew they would be tough. You were fairly warned. But who would have known that finding a loving, nurturing, reliable person to care for your bundle of joy would be so complicated (and boy, is it!). From finding a daycare provider to hiring a nanny, the childcare options seem endless and the process of selecting and hiring a competent caregiver overly complex. Add this to the mix of your loving, maternal bond with your child and your own separation anxiety, and mama, we've got stress!

Since I approach the childcare issue from the other side of the fence, I've sometimes been discouraged by the lengthy process of finding a child to provide care for! I can only empathize with parents who have to tackle the most challenging task by far of working motherhood: finding and securing affordable, quality childcare, as they balance reentry into the workforce with adjusting to postpartum physical and emotional changes. Take heart and know that with a lot of diligence—and a little help from me—you'll find the option that fits your family.

If you've been down the childcare road before, you've probably learned that this is one industry where you truly get what you pay for. Regulations and fees vary from state to state and from arrangement to arrangement, so it's often up to the parents alone to determine the credibility, competency and dependability of each caregiving provider. I know—as if you don't have enough to do! But trust me, a little research now will save you hours of frustration later.

With options ranging in price from as little as $600 to $5,000 or more per month (can you say "sticker shock"?) for full-time care, the cost alone may be the sole factor in determining what will work best for your family. In addition to budgeting, you've also got to consider factors such as family scheduling, your lifestyle, the intensity of care needed and the number (and ages) of the kids who need care. Wading through the terminology of who's who and what's what in the world of early childcare choices and determining the pros and cons of each available option as they relate to the needs of your family is no easy task—but it can be done.

Take Gayle, for example, a friend of mine who works a 9 A.M. to 4 P.M. shift on weekdays as a receptionist in a physician's office. Daycare is a great choice for her because her hours are set, her work week is traditional and her schedule doesn't ever change. She never has to worry about running late at the office, having a work emergency or being called in on the weekends.

On the other end of the spectrum, there's the physician she works for, Dr. Amy Weiss. Her hours are always changing, especially when she is on call. Her schedule varies according to the crises at hand, and she can be called back to work virtually any time of the day or night. In her situation, a daycare arrangement won't work. She needs the type of tailor-made scheduling that only an in-home provider or nanny can provide.

So before you head down and sign up at the first daycare center you pass on the way to work, take some time to review your options and determine your childcare budget. Check out www.sayplanning.com—it has free interactive tools to help you plan steps to accomplish almost anything (any planner at heart, like me, will love it!). Then establish which arrangement best suits the needs of your family. Once you've decided which route you want to take, we'll cover how to make your arrangement work successfully. But first let's review the in-home and out-of-home childcare options available for infants to preschoolers.

| Childcare Option | Average Cost Per Year | Works Best for Working Moms Who . . . |
|---|---|---|
| Center-Based Daycare | $4,020 to $14,225 for full-time care | Need no flexibility in childcare scheduling and have work hours that coincide with the schedule of the daycare center |
| Family Daycare | $4,800 to $6,720 for full-time care | Need minimal flexibility in childcare scheduling and have work hours that coincide with the schedule of the provider |
| Preschool Programs | $12,000 for full-time care | Need no flexibility in childcare scheduling and have work hours that coincide with the schedule of the preschool program |
| Nanny Care | $27,000 to $31,000 for 48-54 hours of care per week | Need maximum flexibility in childcare scheduling and work 10-plus hour days and/or variable nontraditional hours |
| Babysitter | $5.00 to $15.00 per hour | Need maximum flexibility in childcare scheduling and work limited, varying or nontraditional hours |
| Babysitting Co-operative | No Financial Cost | Need minimal care, or set part-time hours and are willing to exchange care with others |

| Childcare Option | Average Cost Per Year | Works Best for Working Moms Who . . . |
|---|---|---|
| Au Pair | $20,800 plus room and board for 45 hours of care a week | Need supplementary care or an extra set of hands on evenings and weekends |
| Family Care | Free and up | Have family with a genuine interest in providing childcare |

## Center-Based Daycare

Center-based daycare centers are one of the most popular types of childcare working mothers choose for their infants and preschoolers. Although fees can vary depending on where you live, on the level of accreditation of the program and on the hours of care that you require, it is often the most affordable option of the early childcare choices.

Many parents find center-based daycare to be a viable option, because programs often accept infants into their programs as early as 6 weeks of age, providing an invaluable service to working mothers who have limited maternity leave and need to get back to work and maintain their pre-delivery income.

Another bonus of center-based care is that it is the best-regulated of the early childcare options. Although regulations do vary from state to state, minimal enforceable standards apply in each state, monitoring staff-child ratios, safety and sanitary standards, teacher training, criminal background investigations for staff, and continuing education requirements for center-based providers. In addition to state regulations, many centers take part in a well-respected voluntary accreditation process through The National Association for the Education of Young Children (NAEYC) that evaluates individual centers according to their NAEYC set of standards (check out

www.naeyc.org). I always recommend NAEYC-accredited facilities to my clients, because of the high standards these centers must adhere to in order to receive and maintain their
accreditation. I agree with Dr. T. Barry Brazelton: "I think one
of the greatest advances to child care was the creation of the
NAEYC Accreditation system, which has helped so much to
raise the quality of programs."[1]

Today, corporately operated centers, such as Bright Horizons, are popping up in industrial parks across the nation. Because they are national chains, they often have more resources
than privately owned centers. Great play structures, plenty of
arts and crafts supplies, and computer learning stations often
line the walls of successful centers.

Whether corporately or privately owned, center-based facilities open and close at specific times, so you'll need to work
around the hours of the center. And if you're late, you'll have
to pay. Sometimes by the minute.

As with any reputable establishment, word travels fast when
there's a good daycare center in town. So if you find a center that
other moms and kids highly recommend, chances are there will
be a waiting list. Start looking very early (a year before enrollment is not unrealistic), and get your name on the center's waiting list. Since most centers have a standing policy that siblings
of currently enrolled students get priority placement, slots for
new children are often extremely limited.

Since center-based daycare centers are the most institutionalized of the childcare choices, chances are your child will
receive a generic type of care. Centers usually dictate your child's
daily schedule and activities, and children are expected to adhere to a very structured routine. Some kids thrive on structure,
but alas, some do not.

Because centers are staffed by numerous providers (and
usually operate 50-52 weeks a year), parents rarely have to be
concerned with securing backup because this is the center's re-

sponsibility. On the flip side, because of the size (and turnover) of the staff, your child may not have the same care provider during his enrollment time. This can be pretty tough on sensitive children who don't handle change well.

Center-based care makes for hassle-free management for moms because the childcare provider isn't your own personal employee. You don't need to worry about finding a replacement if she quits or calls in sick, deal with payroll, provide additional benefits or give day-to-day direction.

Along with the pro of being in an environment that allows your baby to interact with many other children, there are some cons to consider. Germs, for one. Because he will be around lots of kids, your son or daughter will be exposed to lots of illnesses and will likely get sick more often. And of course, when he's sick, you can't send him to daycare. I recently worked with a family who pulled their two children out of center-based care for this reason alone. The kids were constantly sick, and the parents had to take time off for mild illnesses that prevented the children from attending daycare.

Some days, getting yourself together and out of the house on time can be a real hassle. This only multiplies when you have to do the same with a sleepy baby or toddler and figure in an extra stop before getting to work. When you use a center-based facility, you'll need to get your morning routine working like a finely tuned machine (but don't worry—we'll cover that in a chapter to come!).

So you think center-based care may work for your family? Check in with the Nation's Network of Child Care Resource and Referral, www.naccrra.org, and utilize their no-cost research and referral program that can direct you to a licensed center near your home or work. You can also visit the National Association for the Education of Young Children at www.naeyc.org to help you find an accredited, reputable daycare center in your area.

# Home-Based Daycare

Often slightly less costly than center-based care, home-based care is one of the most affordable options for many parents seeking childcare for their young children.

Because programs are usually hosted in the homes of the providers, the comfortable, cozy atmosphere is an attraction for many parents. And unlike corporate centers, which accommodate a large number of children, family-based centers usually service only a few, allowing for more customized care. Children usually receive care from one or two consistent caregivers, which allows them to form a bond with their provider(s).

The very nature of home-based daycares means that the provider can make schedules and programs quite flexible. Usually these providers allow for early drop-off and late pick-up. Some even offer additional evening and weekend care options. I often tell working moms who have to deal with multiple morning drop-offs that a neighborhood home-based daycare can often provide the flexibility they need to make their schedules work. Because center-based facilities usually operate more regimented programs based on strict scheduling, it can often be a real "disruption" if a child gets dropped off five minutes late, or five minutes early, because the teacher-child ratio is thrown off. In home-based settings, the enrollment is smaller, and the provider isn't always walking the "ratio" line.

But here comes the flip side: A daycare operating in someone else's home can come with some pretty big cons. Because the business is located within the caregiver's home, the care provider might be tempted to take care of household and business matters, rather than devote complete attention to the children. Because the care is given in the home, other people (care provider's spouse and older children as well as maintenance or other workers) are often present during daycare hours. Then there is the fact that since providers usually work unsupervised or often with only one other adult, if your childcare provider is sick (or

## Let Your Child's Vote Count

I advise my clients to approach looking for a daycare center the way they'd look for a job. Once you find a center you're interested in, check it out; learn about the program; interview the director and potential providers; check references; and do your research with your local Better Business Bureau and state licensing departments to make sure that the center (and its staff) is up to code. You'll also want to let your child give the daycare center a test drive during a short visit. Observe how she responds to the environment.

Although kids usually prefer to spend their time with Mom rather than at their daycare center, if your child suddenly has more than his usual reluctance about going to (and staying at) his childcare facility, try the following:

1. Ask yourself if there have been any major changes at school or at home. A new teacher at the daycare, a new sibling, a grandparent visiting, a friend that has moved or even a minor illness can significantly impact your child's desire to be left with his childcare provider.

2. Drop in unexpectedly at your daycare center. Make an unannounced visit to see what's going on when you're not there.

3. Volunteer in the classroom. Spending some time observing your child interact with other kids and adults can be quite enlightening. You may be surprised that your relatively "shy" child is quite the social butterfly when you're not around!

4. Notice your child's attitude about his childcare. Does he speak positively about his friends and his teacher? Ask open-ended questions like, "What did you do before snack today?"

5. Talk with the program director to see if she has noticed any issues. Does your child seem withdrawn? Does he do well with the structure of the program, or does he need more or less than what is being provided?

The best advice I can give any parent is to always go with your gut. If you think you need to regularly "spy" on your provider, chances are that you and your child would be better served by another arrangement. But if you identify a concrete factor that may be contributing to your child's change of attitude, if you trust your provider and if you're confident that all is well when you're not there, your child may be experiencing a bout of separation anxiety that will eventually pass.

her children are sick), care can be cancelled with little or no notice, because there is no "staff" to cover such emergencies.

Although regulations widely vary across the United States, most states require the registration and/or licensing of home-based daycares. The National Resource Center for Health and Safety in Child Care and Early Education (check out http://nrc.uchsc.edu/STATES/states.htm) provides a database of state licensure regulations and requirements. Requirements for registration are usually less strict than licensing and although most states require those caring for children other than relatives to be registered and/or licensed by the appropriate governing agency, there are often exemptions (that vary state to state) based on the number and ages of children being cared for in the home. In short, you'll need to do your research to see if the home-based daycare provider is complying with the proper regulations.

Family daycare providers also have the option of voluntary accreditation through the National Association of Family Child Care. This organization sets forth national standards for home-based childcare. Because I feel that there is something to be said for a business that has higher standards than what is required by law, I advise my clients to look for a family daycare that participates in this voluntary accreditation.

Unfortunately, it is common practice for caregivers to take children into their care without obtaining a license or registration when one is required. If a family daycare refuses to comply with state regulation requirements, their in-home daycare is operating illegally. I always tell parents to assume that if a family daycare is not complying with the law, then the providers may not have completed appropriate safety and sanitary training, CPR/First Aid training or criminal background checks. Err on the side of caution when it comes to your kids—always.

You can find accredited family daycare at the National Association of Family Child Care website (www.nafcc.org) through their searchable database. You can also use the resource and referral network of Child Care Aware (check out www.childcare aware.org) to get a no-cost referral to a reputable family daycare in your area.

One last word here about home-based daycare: If the cost of a family daycare program seems too good to be true, it probably is. What starts out as an informal caregiving arrangement for a few children sometimes turns into the illegal operation of a non-compliant daycare—and puts your child at risk. Be sure to check your state regulations and make sure that your provider is compliant.

## Preschool Programs

Not so long ago, I discovered that preschool is the new kinder-garten—no joke! On a recent trip to scout out preschool programs for my nearly three-year-old charge, I was amazed to see that preschools have entered the high-tech world. Computers and cal-culators were available for use, and the digital photography of stu-dents was proudly displayed on the wall of the classroom.

Preschool provides a structured atmosphere, introduces your child to new activities that develop age-appropriate skills, and teaches developmentally appropriate curriculum. But more im-portantly, in preschool your child learns to make it through the day, sans you. Attendance at a reputable preschool prepares your child, socially and academically, for a smooth transition to kin-dergarten. I always encourage parents to choose a program that is in their town or neighborhood so that their kids are enrolled with local children who are likely to be in the same kindergarten class when they enter public school.

If you're looking for a low-maintenance management op-tion as a childcare choice for your 2.9- to nearly 5-year-old, pre-school may be the right choice for you. Preschools are overseen by a director who operates the facility and ensures that the pro-gram and its teachers comply with state regulations and licens-ing requirements. In addition, preschools can get voluntary accreditation through the National Association for the Educa-tion of Young Children. I always advise that parents choose an NAEYC accredited preschool for their children.

Because preschools are educational facilities that have nu-merous teachers on staff, you won't need to worry if the teacher is sick. Subs are always available to cover for your regular teacher. However, if your child is sick, you'll surely need backup. And un-fortunately, if your child isn't potty trained, preschool may not be the right choice. Because of child-staff ratio requirements and sanitation issues, children are usually required to be fully potty trained before entering most preschool programs.

Most programs follow the public school calendar and are closed on holidays and during vacations, so you'll need to work around the schedule of the school. Many preschools do offer extended day programs, in addition to the traditional half day that is customarily offered, which provides a child-care solution for the hours of care needed on either end of the child's school day.

If you think your child may be ready to trade her bottle for a backpack, check into the preschool option. To find a reputable preschool in your area, utilize the searchable database of the National Association for the Education of Young Children (check out www.naeyc.org) or call The Childcare Aware hotline (800-424-2246) to get the number of a local childcare resource and referral agency, which in turn can direct you to licensed preschools in your area.

## What About Co-op Preschools?

If you are nervous about loosening your grip on the reins and letting your child go, consider a co-op preschool that encourages parent participation in the education of their students. Parents sit on the board of the school, volunteer for service and take part in the day-to-day operations of the program. I've been fortunate to have taken part in my former charges' preschool co-ops and have enjoyed helping out and watching them transition to big boyhood. Parent Co-operate Preschools International (check out www.preschools.coop) provides resource and information about co-operative preschools as well as a list of member programs.

## Nanny Care

By far, my favorite childcare option is nanny care. Okay, I admit that I am severely biased—but hear me out. The years I have spent with the kids in my care have been an amazing experience!

To see them grow and develop day in and day out, hour by hour, has created a bond sure to last a lifetime.

While nanny care is the most expensive of the childcare options, it comes with many perks that make it well worth its price tag—just ask any working mother who has one! In addition to being able to hand-select your caregiver, you get to be the boss. Your child is cared for in your home, providing for great convenience and flexibility because your nanny can work around the schedule you determine. Because you are the employer, you set the hours, salary, benefit package, responsibilities, duties and expectations.

For many working moms, hiring a nanny is their dream solution. Provide care for sick children? Check. Provide customized care in a safe, comfortable setting? Check. Necessitate minimal morning effort on Mom's part to get the kids up and out? Check. The children enjoying the comforts of home, having home-cooked meals, naps in their own beds, playtime in their own space and baths in their own tubs? Check! On top of those pros, there is the fact that your child is not exposed to a huge germ pool—which means a healthier child. So let's hear it for nannies! When it comes to kids, there is virtually nothing a nanny can't do to make your childcare dilemma disappear.

Seriously, though, today's professional nannies are educated professionals with a genuine love for children. They usually have extensive experience and early childhood development training. Career nannies take their role and responsibilities seriously and nanny because they want to, not because they have to. They are truly different from a babysitter or au pair (more on that to come!).

Nannies do everything related to the children. Although they are not house cleaners, they pick up after the children, tend to the kids laundry, shop for the kids and do anything related to the care and upbringing of the children. Visit www.nanny.org and read "A Nanny for Your Family" for more information on the roles and responsibilities of a professional nanny.

Of course, there is a cost involved in nanny care, but remember that the more kids you have in nanny care, the more cost-effective it becomes. Because you pay per family, rather than per child, families with two or more children find that it can actually be *less* costly to hire a nanny than to pay for two full-time slots in a daycare. One parent I consulted with did the calculations, and by the time she paid for daycare for her infant and full-day preschool for her older child, hiring a single child-care provider saved her both time and money.

Although the perks of having a nanny are nearly endless, there are downsides, too. Because nannies work inside the homes of their employers, some working moms don't like the loss of privacy that comes with the nanny territory. One former nanny employer put it like this: "I have to be professional and keep professional boundaries all day at work—it's the last thing I want to do in my own home. And I certainly don't want to have to panic if my underwear is left in the corner of the bathroom after my shower."

Because a nanny works unsupervised and is often the only adult in the home all day, you need to be sure that you hire a self-motivated caregiver. Isolation for the nanny and the children can be an issue if your nanny isn't a naturally social butterfly, though if you have an outgoing nanny (like me!) you can kiss your worries in that department goodbye. My former employer used to chuckle when she'd pop home on a midsummer day and find a full barbeque in swing with me, my charges and all the neighborhood kids having an all-out playparty. To avoid a lack of socialization, encourage your nanny to take your child to local classes or to the park, or to host playgroups on a regular basis.

Beyond embracing your lack of total privacy, you'll need to accept the challenge of employing a quality nanny. You'll have to manage your nanny and become a legitimate employer. You'll need to pay taxes, and in some cases offer benefits such as health insurance, vacation and sick time. GTM Associates (check out www.GTM.com) is a great resource that specializes in guiding nanny employers through this process. As well, *How to Hire a Nanny* by Guy Maddalone (GTM's CEO) is a great resource for nanny employers, or those thinking about the nanny option.

Because of the lack of supervision in this particular workplace—your home—it is nearly impossible to regulate the nanny profession. Although placement agencies are required in most states to hold a license to operate, individual nannies are not nationally regulated. Voluntary certification, however, is available for nannies through the International Nanny Association (INA). They have a member list on their website—you'll see my name there (check out www.nanny.org). So if you think a nanny may be right for your family, visit INA's website or that of the Alliance of Premier Nanny Agencies (check out www. theapna.com) and search for a member placement agency in your area.

Nanny placement agencies help screen nannies and can be an invaluable resource; but if paying a referral fee is out of your budget, the International Nanny Association has member businesses that will screen your selected candidate for you. Although it may be appealing to hire off the books or hire an illegal immigrant, or to find and attempt to screen a nanny on your own, utilizing a reputable nanny placement agency that will guide you through the process and help screen your potential nanny is worth the cost. Background checks, reference checks (although I advise parents to do a separate check on their own), driving-record checks, as well as a statement of good health, in-depth interviews and a replacement policy are all part of the package that a quality agency provides. If you are going to find a nanny on your own, be sure to screen carefully. Require a driving record and certificate of good health, do a background check and always personally check at least three references.

## Babysitters

Babysitters are a great childcare option for working moms who need limited but regular childcare coverage. Maybe you wait tables a few nights a week and need someone to cover the time between when you leave and when your husband gets home, or maybe you and your spouse need a night on the town after your hard day at work. Babysitters provide that "as needed" type of childcare service upon which many working moms have come to depend.

Since you're the boss, you set the schedule and you choose the provider. Easy, right? Not always. Babysitters usually work on an occasional basis, often have no formal training and don't consider childcare their profession. They see babysitting as a secondary source of income to supplement their full-time job or are students who see babysitting as a job that they can work around their class schedules. This means that your babysitter probably has limited availability, so you'll need to book well in advance once you find a sitter you trust.

Babysitters are hired to supervise and care for the children in the home. Don't expect your babysitter to prepare meals, do laundry or other non-essential tasks, or you'll come home disappointed.

The best way to find a reputable babysitter is by word of mouth. Network with other moms—find out who they use for childcare. Or you might try putting a listing on your church or community bulletin board to widen your search for quality providers. Teachers and youth workers can often provide names of mature young people who may fit the bill as babysitter. You can also check out websites such as www.sittercity.com that provide searchable résumés of babysitters with ratings from families who have used their services. You can usually find dozens of postings from babysitters in your area on these sites.

I always advise parents to look for a sitter that has taken a babysitting course through the American Red Cross and to be sure that she has current CPR/First Aid certification. Parents should also personally check references beforehand and then observe their sitter in action before leaving her alone with their baby.

## Babysitting Co-operative

Working mothers in major metropolitan areas are getting on the babysitting co-operative bandwagon. Co-operatives, or co-ops, are usually neighborhood- or interest-based, so chances are, you know the other parents well. Co-operatives are a great option for parents whose budget says that they need to barter for, rather than pay for, childcare.

I have a friend in New York who learned of a babysitting co-operative in her high-rise apartment building. Because she was a writer and was able to work out her own schedule, she loved having other parents in the building with whom she could swap childcare. "To Anna, it's like going upstairs to play with her little friends. To me, it's much-needed time to get my work done—in silence."

Many co-operatives use a points system, so you need to put points in, in order to take points out; you give care to get care. Working moms who work part time (or make their own schedule) find that teaming up with another working mom who works an opposite shift is a great childcare option and a win-win for both.

To see if a babysitting co-operative is currently available in your area, Google "babysitting co-op" with your town's name, and see what comes up. If you find one, don't jump on board before asking for the rules and requirements for membership and for references. You can also ask around, since co-ops are common among park playgroups, in churches and among "parents of preschoolers" groups.

If a co-operative babysitting arrangement sounds like it's something that may work for you and there isn't one presently available for you to take part in, think about starting your own! Check out www.babysittingcoop.com, which provides resources for and information on how to start your own co-op.

And don't forget to check into Mother's Day Out programs (often associated with churches) if you just need to work a couple of days a week. Many of them are excellent, and most children, from my friend Becky's experience, love going.

## Au Pair

The au pair program is a cultural exchange program that is regulated through the U.S. Department of State. Through the program, students from abroad come to the United States to experience American life with a host family in exchange for up to 45 hours per week of childcare.

Although the au pair program is regulated by the U.S. government through 12 approved au pair placement agencies, the skill sets and childcare experience vary greatly from au pair to au pair. Although au pairs need 200 or more documented hours of childcare experience to have a child under age two placed in their care, currently au pairs cannot provide care in homes with infants under three months of age, unless a responsible adult is always home.

While an au pair is in your home, she is not your employee. She is in the United States to experience American life as part of your family. You'll need to provide her with vacation time, as well as transportation to and from her educational courses. You are also expected to provide her with an experience of authentic American family life. But it's not a one-way street. Here's what one parent had to say about her family's experience with their au pair: "We got to experience the customs and language of another culture, from the comforts of our home. But we also got to experience language and cultural barriers and feeling like we've taken on a college student to parent as we dealt with her intense desire to experience city life first hand."

So remember, although the au pair program is often marketed to American parents as a cheap alternative form of childcare, it is marketed to potential candidates as a great way to see America! When the parties meet, there is sometimes confusion over the expectations of duties and responsibilities. Au pairs are *not* nannies—they have not necessarily chosen childcare as their profession. Their skill set and experience may not line up with what you want or require—but then again, it might! Just be sure to do your homework ahead of time, and be sure that you and your au pair candidate are on the same page.

If you think an au pair may be your childcare solution, visit the U.S. Department of State's website (see http://exchanges.state.gov) and download the au pair brochure.

## Family Member

They're family, right? What can go wrong? Well, quite a bit, actually. The success of this childcare option definitely depends on the individual family and their unique arrangement.

It's obviously wonderful if you have a family member who is genuinely interested in providing the care you need for your child. This type of arrangement can be especially beneficial to everyone involved, as it facilitates a life-long, strong family bond between the caregiver and the child. Not only will your child get lots of love and attention from someone who already loves him, but his care provider is someone who is genuinely concerned with his health and well-being.

All this sounds great so far, right? What can go wrong? Well, in short, *plenty*.

I certainly don't want to burst your bubble or minimize the successes that many families have with this arrangement, but the realities of working with family are still there. Family members can often be hard to manage. They may start out with great intentions and then decide that they've taken on too much.

Not too long ago, I got a frantic call from one mom who shared her story with me: "I had a nanny all lined up, but at the last minute my parents decided they really wanted to help out and care for the kids. Now, three weeks later, they tell me that it's too much. I need another nanny right now! What should I do?"

My advice to her? "Contact a babysitting service to cover the next few days while you re-evaluate your options. If you decide to go with another family arrangement, put together a basic agreement that outlines the schedule, compensation, duties and responsibilities; then agree to review it every three months to be sure everyone is still on the same page."

One last word of advice regarding the family arrangement: Although a relative may refuse to take payment from you, be sure to compensate her with some form of gratitude and small gifts that you can afford. As a working mom, you know that being appreciated goes a long way, and expressions of sincere appreciation are sometimes more than enough payment.

## Making It Work

You've sorted through your options, and now you have a handle on what you want to do. You've located your Mary Poppins, Daycare Dream Team or other perfect potential arrangement. Now what?

Once you've settled on a provider that looks promising, here's what you'll need to do.

1. *Interview.* Whether you've chosen a daycare center, babysitter or nanny, take some time to get to know your potential candidate.

   • When interviewing for childcare arrangements outside of the home, be sure to ask:

     ♦ Does the center have an opening?
     ♦ What are the hours of operation and the fees?

- Do they have an open-door policy so that you can stop in any time?
- What is the policy for closings? Holidays? Vacations?
- What is the policy for caring for sick children?
- How are the children grouped? By age?
- How do they monitor children? What is the ratio of children to provider?
- Are they licensed and/or registered and accredited?
- What are the educational background and experiences of the caregivers?
- What is the philosophy of the program? Is it schedule-oriented, or are the activities more child-directed?

- When interviewing for in-home childcare arrangements, be sure to ask:

  - Why are you interested in working with children?
  - Are you able to fulfill the required duties and responsibilities, as detailed in our job description?
  - Can you work the hours specified for the salary offered?
  - What is your experience and educational background?
  - Why did you leave your last job?
  - What is your discipline philosophy? What do you do when a child throws a temper-tantrum? Do you use the time-out method of discipline?
  - How would you stimulate my child both mentally and socially? What can you contribute to his growth and development?
  - What would your average day with my child be like?

2. *Check References.* Make personal contact with others who have used the services of the provider. Contact a minimum of three references and always ask if they'd be comfortable using the caregiver's services again.

3. *Observe.* Set up a time to see your caregiver in action. Whether you schedule a visit at your home or a visit to an onsite provider, be sure to take note of how the caregiver interacts with children and whether the environment is clean, safe, stimulating.

4. *Give it a go.* Have a trial day to give your child the opportunity to try out the childcare arrangement; then evaluate your choice based on how she responds to the new environment.

5. *Sign a contract.* Whether you decide on a formal contract or a written work agreement, be sure to get something in writing that outlines the duties, responsibilities, hours, financial obligations, and policies and procedures that govern your arrangement. Be sure to check to see if it includes a trial period—if not, ask if you can add it in.

6. *Meet regularly.* Plan on meeting with your provider weekly for the first few months and monthly thereafter. Even if it's just for a few moments during drop-off or during a brief evening phone call, schedule a time to talk about everything pertinent to the care of your child.

7. *Keep the lines of communication open.* Foster an environment of openness and honesty. Give feedback to your provider, and ask for her input on issues relating to the care of your child.

8. *Show professional courtesy.* Treat your provider as the professional that she is. Remember, she has a life outside of your child, so being punctual and professional will go a long way toward displaying appreciation for the care she is providing to your child.

9. *Give bonuses, raises or gifts to show appreciation.* If you're looking for a sure-fire way to let your caregiver know she is appreciated, an occasional gift goes a long way. It need not be extravagant—even a card with a drawing from your child or homemade cookies will show that you value your provider.

## SCENE 4: TAKE 2
### On the Phone

**Cheryl** (*to Paula*): Did I tell you that Ken said I could bring Addyson to work for the first few weeks? I am so relieved.

**Paula:** No, you didn't. That's great news! You must be thrilled.

**Cheryl:** Really, it is great. I am in the midst of my search for long-term childcare, and this gives me a bit more time.

**Paula:** Yeah, you mentioned the other day that you had begun the childcare search. Any luck?

**Cheryl:** There are so many options, but I really think center-based care would work best for our family. Sean and I both work normal hours, so we don't need to worry about flexibility, and it fits our budget. Plus, Mom has agreed to watch Addyson two days a week to give her some "grandma 'n' me" time. For the other three days, I think Addyson will benefit from being around other kids and bonding with other adults. Little Lamb Daycare, in the church up the road, looks really good. I have an interview set up next week.

**Paula:** Wow, you've really thought this through and found what works best for your family. That's great.

**Cheryl:** It sure is, but boy, did finding a practically perfect arrangement take a lot more time and effort than I ever would have imagined! Still, I can't wait to check out the center in person.

## WHY WAS CHERYL SO CONFIDENT IN HER NEW POTENTIAL CHILDCARE ARRANGEMENT?

- *She understood the needs of her family.* Take the time to figure out your budget and the needs of your family.

- *She examined her options.* Investigate your options and decide which option best matches your family's needs and budget.

- *She went through the process.* Although the process is time-consuming, realize the importance of doing your homework, interviewing potential providers and understanding what you're getting into before making a decision.

- *She was creative with her arrangement.* To balance a strong sense of family with a quality social experience, consider multiple options to achieve your desired outcome.

**Q:** *I'm returning to work after the birth of my second child. I can't believe it, but it seems easier to leave my infant than my toddler. How can I get my toddler to adjust to his new caregiving situation?*

**A:** You've already hinted that you understand an important aspect of beginning a new childcare situation: that there is a time of adjustment. If you are truly happy with your childcare arrangement, the best thing you can do to help your toddler adjust is to convey your confidence in his caregiver. Keeping goodbyes short and sweet and resisting the urge to linger during drop-off will convey to him that you are leaving him in safe hands. And however tempting it may be, never sneak out without saying goodbye. Developing a consistent, predictable morning routine as well as a standard drop-off procedure will also go a long way in helping your child to feel safe and secure while he is in the care of another.

**Q:** *My mother-in-law really wants to be the primary caregiver for our new baby when I go back to work. How can I politely tell her no?*

**A:** When telling people something they don't want to hear, the news is usually more easily swallowed when positive language is used in conjunction with a solid "I" statement. So when your mother-in-law shares with you her desire to be your full-time childcare provider, an appropriate gentle response would be, "Wow, that is a really generous offer, but we've already made [or are in the works of securing, or are still sorting out] our childcare arrangements. I am glad that you live so close and can be an active part of the baby's life. I am really appreciative of the offer."

**Q:** *I am a divorced mother of two, and I have a hard time when my children spend the weekends with my ex-husband and his new wife. How can I be sure my kids are safe when they are in their care?*

**A:** It's been said that one of the best gifts a parent can give her child is to love and respect the child's other parent. Even in the case of divorce, it is crucial for your children that you maintain a positive attitude and decent relationship with your ex. If you have legitimate concerns about what goes on in his home while your children are visiting, set up a time to speak with your ex in a neutral location, when you are calm and the children are not around. To help ease the transition for the children, try to work out some basic guidelines, house rules and behavior expectations that you both agree to adhere to for the sake of the kids. Of course, if you are truly concerned that your children may be in an unsafe environment or are possibly being abused, contact local law enforcement and your lawyer about what steps to take to limit their contact with a potentially dangerous or abusive parent.

**Q:** *I've found a really great daycare facility. My gut says it's a perfect fit. Do I really need to spend my time checking references?*

**A:** Checking references for any childcare provider is an absolute must. Under no circumstances should you leave your child with a caregiver whom you have not thoroughly checked out. Phone references to a caregiver's present and previous clients, educational confirmation, a criminal background investigation and driver's license checks all provide you with essential information on a potential childcare provider. You can rest easy knowing that your child is in good hands *only after* you've done your homework and have proof that you've made a good choice.

**Q:** *My nanny has been taking care of our toddler for eight months. Recently she began crying when our nanny arrives in the morning. I call a few minutes after leaving and I hear her playing happily. Should I be concerned?*

**A:** Children often go through a stage when separation anxiety is intense—they don't want to be away from their parents. Changes in routine or family situations or time away from their regular caregiver due to vacation can also trigger the "I don't want you" syndrome. Even after kids have become truly comfortable with their caregiver, they can still temporarily regress, attempting to reject their nanny to see if they are truly loved and if their environment is really safe and secure. Older toddlers often cry for Mommy, especially if they believe their efforts will result in Mommy staying home to take care of them. So if you have complete confidence in your caregiver, chances are, things are fine. You can always drop in unexpectedly or call a few times during the day to be sure your child is doing well.

**Q:** *My mother watches my son three days a week. How can I get her to understand the importance of following our routine and sticking to my childrearing preferences?*

**A:** Begin by telling your mom how much you appreciate her caring for your son and by expressing your desire for her to continue to play this important role in his life. Then gently explain to her that in order for her to continue to do so, you need to develop some consistency in rules and routines for your child. Brainstorm and come up with some things that you can both agree to adhere to; then share with her any non-negotiable rules or routines that you need her to enforce. Thank her again for helping you to create the best caregiving situation for your son, and agree to keep each other informed about how the new arrangement is working.

# 5

# GOT MILK?

*At the Office on a Conference Call*

**Colleen** (*to Katie, as she presses the speakerphone mute button*): Wasn't this call slated to end at 4:30?

**Katie** (*sarcastically*): Yeah, I know. Welcome back to the corporate world.

**Colleen:** I mean, really. Do they forget we're on the east coast and that most people don't have childcare after 5 P.M.?

**Katie** (*smiling, handing her a tissue*): Or have babies they need to feed.

**Colleen** (*looking down*): Oh, great. Just what I need. Two milk-stained bull's-eyes to go along with the black eyes I have from sleep deprivation. I'm telling you, these things need a shut-off valve.

**Katie:** And you need to go home. I'll wrap up here and send you a memo tonight.

**Colleen:** No, I'll stick it out. I've really got to get on board with this project.

Tired, drained (literally!) and feeling ever so conflicted, you've survived (barely) the commute on your first day back to work. You even managed to give yourself a pep talk about the importance of giving "getting back into the groove" your best shot as you drove the long and lonely car ride (okay, it's a 10-minute drive, but today it felt like an eternity).

You've arrived in one piece. Well, make that two pieces: you and your electric pumping companion. You've made the "welcome back" rounds (smile, show picture, nod, smile, show picture, nod), and you are now ready to settle into what used to be your cozy desk chair (you've since developed an intense affection for chairs that rock and pair well with an ottoman). You would be feeling like the savvy business woman you once were if it weren't for one, make that two, small . . . um, make that *large* problems: a pair of uncooperative and decidedly unprofessional-looking breasts.

The days of "perky" are sadly over, and your two former friends are now swollen, sore, full, engorged and drippy. It's as if they're displaying total dissatisfaction with their new babyless environment and protesting wildly. Which means you are doubly distraught.

You think pulling out a photo of adorable Lucas and setting it on your desk might help, but that only causes your milk factory to start churning on autopilot. You thank God for breast pads (even though, at times, it looks like you have a couple of four-inch whoopee pies stuffed under your shirt) and attempt to focus on anything but missing your baby.

## Bare Necessities

If you've decided that you prefer to feed your baby breast milk instead of formula, you've probably already realized that pumping at work is going to require some careful planning and advance preparation. If you've been practicing using your breast pump at home, the good news is that you've probably discovered that the compact motorized device you'll be toting to and from the office can generate enough power to jump-start your car if you happen to have a dead battery during a winter storm. The bad news is that you'll need to carry it to work, every day, along with an arsenal of other supplies, if you want the remote-breastfeeding arrangement to work.

Okay, I'm exaggerating—sort of. But if you've yet to consider using a high-voltage pump with all its accessories, I'll walk you through it. Just pull up a chair, hoist those fully loaded "girls" up on a desk (to take a break from hauling them around) and pay close attention.

Besides taking care to keep your breasts moisturized with a quality lanolin ointment (which is safe for babies if ingested), the most important thing you'll need is a good quality electric pump. While there are many makes and models to choose from, I recommend a hospital- or professional-grade model that is designed for regular, daily use. Many of my clients love the Medela Pump in Style model because of its discreet carrying case and its built-in storage cooler—not to mention its unmatched, adjustable, simultaneous suction power (if this is suddenly sounding like a car commercial, just bear with me). Seriously, if you're looking for an electric pump that really does the job (and looks more like a classy shoulder bag or backpack than a car battery), this is your best option.

Because a good pump can cost anywhere between $130 and $300, many working mothers prefer to rent hospital-grade pumps from their local pharmacy or hospital. You may also want to check with your insurance carrier or employer to see if they offer any lactation benefits such as discounted pumps, lactation consultation or other nursing incentives. Some hospitals now even offer free follow-up breastfeeding assessments—just to be sure that you and your baby are thriving.

As if your mornings aren't crazy enough, you'll also need to remember to take all the doodads with you that make pump operation possible. I met with a client who actually had to purchase a spare set of accessories for the car, because after sterilizing all the breast shields and bottles at night, she'd get halfway to work only to realize that she'd left them on the counter at home! I often advise newly work-and-pump moms to make themselves a little checklist for all the parts (tubing, breast shields, membranes, valves, collection bottles, ice packs) that they need to take to work, and to develop a routine for washing the pump parts and packing their bags. Until it feels automatic, you might write out a schedule to post on the fridge to keep you on track!

Taking care of your breasts will also become an added chore. From clogged milk ducts, to breast infections, your breastfeeding adventure can give you some pretty painful memories if you aren't careful. Expressing a bit of milk after pumping goes a long way toward preventing cracked nipples. Other preventive measures include getting rest, drinking lots of water and wearing loose-fitting bras. Also, don't go too long between nursing or pumping, or the milk will back up and clog your ducts. You know this has happened when you get a very red, warm, hard spot on your breast. If this happens, take a warm bath and call the doctor as soon as possible. If you need antibiotics, you'll want to start them as soon as possible. Like a bladder infection, time quickly worsens the pain, but antibiotics can do wonders to ease your suffering.

I also encourage my breastfeeding clients to bring paper towels (I love the Viva ones that really do feel like cloth), antibacterial wipes, microwavable sterilization bags, dish soap and a drying rack to tidy up themselves and their miscellaneous accessories after a pumping session. Depending on your work setup, you may have a comfy nursing room that has a designated sink and fridge, snacks, magazines and bottled water for your use; or you may be confined to your office to pump. In this case, you'll have to use the bathroom to rinse your supplies, then store your milk in an insulated cooler or a community fridge.

If you don't have an office with a door but live instead in cubicle world, retail land or factory town, check with your employer to see if there is an unused room (or closet with an outlet) that can be turned into a nursing room. You won't get help if you don't ask for it. Or perhaps you've got a colleague who'll let you use her private office to pump while she's away on her lunch hour. Another creative solution is to bring in a room divider and a chair to place in the bathroom to create your own nursing-mom sanctuary.

Whatever your limited workplace circumstances, remember that sitting in a stall on an open toilet seat to pump is not your only option. In fact, it's the easiest thing in the world to pump in your minivan! Get yourself a car adapter, recline the seat and listen to your favorite music as you pump. Or call and check on your baby! It may not be luxurious, but it is private and peaceful.

One last word of advice—and perhaps it almost goes without saying: A cute photo of your baby will help your milk flow. One mother I worked with even brought along a onesie to work that still smelled of her little guy so that her senses would be completely engulfed in everything baby. And it helped her feel close to him and miss him just a bit less, too!

## Soaring Along the Milky Way

Even though after the first few days of pumping at work you may be ready to throw in the towel, give yourself some time to ride out the emotional ups and downs of your strange new routine. You're bound to feel a mixture of guilt, resentment, jealousy and worry about not feeding your baby from the source—so be prepared. But then again, you may feel a bit of relief that your breast pads don't soak through as often, because there is no crying baby to stimulate your milk flow. Still, it's likely that you'll feel physical discomfort as your body adapts to its new "feeding" schedule.

One of the most difficult emotions I see pump-at-work mothers struggle with is feeling torn. One mother explained it like this: "I want to give 100 percent and show that I am a team player at work, but staying a few minutes late to tie up a project is not just staying a few minutes late anymore. It means leaky breasts, a baby that's hungry and a caregiver who is almost out of my milk. I feel like I am constantly forced to choose between advancing my career or feeding my baby." Another mother who works at a law firm reported, "My supervisors and coworkers just don't understand that my days of after-hours functions are over. I sometimes feel like I am getting penalized for not going to dinner with a client, and it's not even during working hours. Don't they get that I have a baby to feed?"

Mothers who successfully navigate the difficulties of pumping while working credit a good support system. One mom shared with me, "Once Jen and I realized we were both pump-at-work moms, an instant friendship was created." Finding some "breast friends" or "bosom buddies" can be your greatest source of support.

## Milking Out

It won't be long before you've worked out a pumping schedule that makes both your boss and your breasts happy. You've figured out when work slows down and can escape for those desperately needed moments. You've scheduled your lunch (and breaks) to coordinate with when your breasts need to be emptied. And you've figured out precisely when your last pumping of the day needs to occur to allow enough time to build up your supply for a "real" feeding when you return home.

But what happens when you are in a meeting that's running late and you absolutely can't hold off pumping any longer? You've seen the "Got Milk?" ads, right? Well, these are the moments when you feel like you've got enough milk to feed an entire country of babies and are eager to do so.

## Book Review: *The Milk Memos*

*The Milk Memos: How Real Moms Learned to Mix Business with Babies—and How You Can, Too* by Cate Colbrun-Smith and Andrea Serrette

If you've not read the book *The Milk Memos* and you are a pumping mom, you've got to take a lunch break and pick up a copy. It's a must-read for all nursing moms. *The Milk Memos* provides humorous insight, practical tips and real-life stories about balancing work and nursing motherhood. Unlike most breastfeeding books, *The Milk Memos* hits on it all: the emotional ups and downs, the physical demands, the office politics and even how to deal with those who just don't have a clue. *The Milk Memos* is an entertaining book that is sure to make you laugh, sure to make you cry and sure to show you how (and empower you) to successfully do it all.

Let's just say you wouldn't be the first mom I know who has hit the mute button during a conference call to squeeze in some pumping time, or who has boldly announced that she needs to excuse herself to "express her milk" (believe me, nothing clears a room of male executives faster!). But there are more subtle ways of getting out of some of the sticky situations that arise from pumping at work, such as "I need 10 minutes to tend to something," which is always a good segue into a quick departure. Others have found that being up-front with their employers about their needs can also help: "I was up-front with my boss about my desire to breastfeed, so when I say 'I need a few minutes,' she knows I really do need a few minutes. And now!"

Many nursing mothers (or "milk mamas" as some of my lactating friends call themselves) get amazingly proficient with multitasking. One friend shared with me: "I'm blessed to have an office with a door. Oftentimes I just put a blanket over me while I pump and find I can also check email, adjust my calendar, read briefs and edit reports. No problem."

Having a stockpile of breast milk in your freezer at home gives most moms a wonderful feeling of security. If for any reason she can't get to her baby or becomes ill, there's plenty of nourishment for her caregiver to give her child in the meantime. Also, many babies will take formula in a pinch, and it's probably a good idea to have a can on hand, for backup, if needed.

Though feeding your baby breast milk can be, without a doubt, a real hassle, for many moms it is well worth it. Pumping can give a working mom a feeling of connectedness to her child and a sense of pride in knowing she's giving of herself to nourish her child, even when she's not at home. Nursing (or pumping) also helps get your uterus and your figure back in shape. A nursing baby drinks about 500 of your calories a day—not a bad way to lose your pregnancy weight in fairly short order.

So you think you're ready to be a lean, not-so-mean, milk-making machine? Take this true-or-false quiz to test your lactating knowledge.

1. With breastfeeding, breast size really matters (I threw that in to see if you are paying attention!).
2. Breastfeeding reduces the mother's risk of ovarian and breast cancer.
3. Breastfed babies are less likely to be sick, reducing your time away from the office.
4. Breastfed babies are less likely to have ear infections.
5. According to every leading health organization, breast milk is best.

Answers: 1. False. 2. True. 3. True. 4. True. 5. True

## SCENE 5: TAKE 2
### *At the Office on a Conference Call*

**Colleen** (*to Katie, pressing the speakerphone mute button*): Wasn't this call slated to end at 4:30?

**Katie** (*sarcastically*): Yeah, I know. Welcome back to the corporate world.

**Colleen:** I mean, *really*. Do they forget we're on the east coast and that most people don't have childcare after 5 P.M.?

**Katie** (*smiling, handing her a tissue*): Or have babies they need to feed.

**Colleen** (*looking down*): Oh, great. This is just what I need. Two milk-stained bull's-eyes to go along with the black eyes I have from sleep deprivation. I'm telling you, these things need a shut-off valve. I really need to jump away from this call, as you can plainly see, unless you want some breast milk to lighten your coffee there. I'm about to blow! Can you fill me in later?

**Katie** (*laughing*): Sure, go home. I'll wrap up here and send you a memo tonight.

**Colleen:** Thanks, Katie. Actually, me, my breasts and my baby thank you.

---

## WHY WAS COLLEEN SO CONFIDENT IN HER ROLE AS A NURSING- AND WORKING-MOTHER?

- *She wasn't afraid to accept special treatment.* You need the help of trusted coworkers to make pumping at work successful—so don't be afraid to ask for it!

- *She had a sense of humor about her situation.* Laughter is the best stress-reducing medicine!

- *She found an alternative way to get her work done.* Have a backup plan to get the information you need to complete your work.

- *She showed appreciation to her coworkers.* People like to help people who are grateful for the assistance they receive.

**Q:** *I've heard that drinking a glass of wine while breastfeeding is safe if you pump and dump your milk, and then allow them to refill before feeding your baby. Is this true?*

**A:** Although the American Academy of Pediatrics says that an occasional small alcoholic drink is permissible for breastfeeding mothers, on the whole, nursing moms are discouraged from drinking alcohol while breastfeeding because it becomes concentrated in breast milk and can inhibit milk production.[1] If you do decide to have a celebratory drink, the Academy advises avoiding breastfeeding for two hours after you indulge.

**Q:** *Is it safe to get a flu shot while breastfeeding?*

**A:** The Vaccination Services of America states that the flu shot is safe for pregnant women, breastfeeding mothers and their infants.

**Q:** *How many more calories do I need to eat while breastfeeding?*

**A:** Healthy breastfeeding mothers who consume between 1,800 and 2,200 additional calories per day maintain an adequate milk supply.[2]

However, if your milk supply is coming well, don't force yourself to eat more than you are truly hungry for, as this is also probably nature's way of giving you a jump-start toward weight loss and regaining your shapely figure.

*Q: While at work, how many times a day should I be pumping?*

**A:** The general rule of thumb is that you should express your milk each time you would normally be feeding your child. This usually means pumping every two to three hours. If your schedule can't accommodate lengthy stints away from your desk, remember that pumping even a little will help maintain your milk supply.

*Q: There is another new mom at my work who doesn't breastfeed or pump. She is constantly making comments to me like, "How can you stand the inconvenience of having to stop what you are doing to pump?" What is the best way to handle her comments?*

**A:** Mothers who have never breastfed often have many misconceptions about the breastfeeding process. The next time your coworker offers her unsolicited advice, thank her for her concern, offer a brief explanation, such as "Breastfeeding is the right choice for me," and direct the conversation to another parenting topic that feels less invasive to you.

*Q: My sister is the mother of two. She breastfed her first and bottle-fed her second. She keeps discouraging me from breastfeeding because she says that breastfed babies are more clingy and demanding than bottle-fed babies. Is there any truth to this?*

**A:** This myth has its root in the belief that a breastfed baby becomes more dependent on his mother and that an overly dependent baby will turn into an overly dependent child. The truth is, regardless of feeding methods, all babies will eventually develop their independence and become confident children, provided their environment fosters and embraces curiosity, exploration and self-discovery. Independence in any child has more to do with his developmental stage than his eating habits.

*Q: Is breastfeeding really the cause of sagging breasts?*

**A:** Breastfeeding or not, your breasts will probably sag somewhat after a pregnancy or two. Unfortunately, sagging breasts are due to genetics and gravity, not breastfeeding. Relax, ladies—this is what push-up bras and well-fitting lingerie were created for! (And trust me, as long as you make your breasts available, your husband will be delighted with them in any shape, size or form!)

Still, I know that many women get depressed that their postpregnancy bodies look more like a bowl full of Jell-O than their former selves. It takes *time*, so be patient! Nursing, working out with a DVD for postpartum mothers and lugging around all that baby equipment will have you back in shape in no time. Even so, you may have stretch marks and looser skin: Take them in stride—you've earned your "stripes of motherhood"—and move on with your life. Your husband will continue to adore you if you continue to feel confident about your body.

After you've had all the children you'd like to have, you may want to save for a tummy tuck, breast lift or lipo someday to help restore your post-mommy body a bit more. But most women and their husbands make peace with the new shape that pregnancy brings. They find that the love and the amazing experience they share together as parents more than make up for how time and pregnancy transform Mommy's body.

# 6

# BEFORE- AND AFTER-SCHOOL CHILDCARE CHOICES

**SCENE 6: TAKE 1**
*In the Living Room*

**Gina-Marie** (*to Donna*): You know, once Bella went to school, I thought my childcare worries would be over. But actually, they seem to have gotten worse.

**Donna:** Worse? She's in school most of the day.

**Gina-Marie** (*irritated*): Yeah! That's the problem. Most of the day. Now I can't find care for the limited time I do need care after school and before I get home from work.

**Donna:** What about the daycare program she's attended up until now?

**Gina-Marie:** They don't do after-school care, only full-day programs.

**Donna:** What about her school? They must offer something.

**Gina-Marie:** There is a wait list. I don't know what to do! My options are so limited, and though I tried to change my work schedule, I just couldn't.

**Donna:** You can't be the only one in this boat, and certainly you aren't the first.

**Gina-Marie:** I guess not, but I just can't seem to figure out
where my other options are hiding.

---

You've been looking forward to the time when you would no
longer need full-time childcare, the season when your daughter
would be enjoying her time at school, learning new skills and
making new friends, while you could work without worry and
keep more of the money you earn, since paying for full-time
childcare wouldn't be needed anymore.

Perhaps you spent the summer before kindergarten preparing for the first day of school: shopping for clothes, a new lunch
box and the other gadgets and gizmos that mark the big day.
Your daughter is officially a big girl now.

And you're officially entering into The Childcare Gap.

The Childcare Gap is the gap of time from two or three in
the afternoon—when the kids get out of school—until about five
or six in the evening, when most parents return from their day
at work. It's only a few hours, so finding childcare to cover this
time should be easy, right? Wrong. Securing quality childcare
for such a limited time can be tough. The 20 or so hours of care
a week needed are just enough to need a consistent arrangement,
but are often not enough hours to secure a slot in a quality program, or enough hours/pay for a caregiver to be willing to sacri-
fice their personal schedule to commit to a regular in-home
childcare arrangement.

Then, of course, there's the transportation issue, which often limits your Childcare Gap options. Say you've found the perfect program across town from the elementary school. Now you
need to figure out how to get your child there. Does the school
offer transportation? Does the program have a pick-up service?

As you can see, finding gap coverage has its challenges—but they aren't insurmountable. Let's take a look at the chart below, which lists several viable childcare options for working mothers who are looking for gap coverage. It shows the average cost of each option and offers suggestions regarding what will work best for a variety of needs.

| Childcare Options | Cost | Works Best for Working Moms Who . . . |
|---|---|---|
| Licensed Childcare Programs | $449 to $7,160 per year, per child | Have a workday that ends before the program does |
| Exempt Programs | Free and up Usually paid per visit | Have older, independent children that need basic supervisory care |
| In-Home Childcare | **Nanny:** $12 to $20 per hour **Babysitters:** $5 to $15 per hour **Au pair:** Room and board plus $140 weekly stipend **Relative, friend or family:** Free and up | Need flexible coverage and want customized childcare |
| Self-Care | Free | Have an independent, responsible child age 12 and up |
| Combination | Depends on arrangements | Have a great network of reliable support and a limited budget |

Now that you have a general idea of your options, let's explore each one a bit more.

# Licensed Childcare Programs

If you are looking for a structured, traditional after-school program for your youngster, a licensed childcare program may be just the ticket, and the good news is that you may not have to look too far to find one. Many elementary schools operate what is commonly referred to as an "extended day" program. Although it's usually a business entity that operates separately from the school—and has its own director and staff—the school *hosts* the program, which provides care for children after school and into the early evening hours, when parents get off work.

"The after-school program was really an answer to my prayers," one working mom said. "Although I only work part time three days a week, finding care for those days and hours was daunting. The childcare center wanted a minimum number of enrollment hours—which I couldn't guarantee—so my child didn't qualify. The in-home providers I researched also wanted a guaranteed number of billable hours. Then, though our extended family is happy to pitch in now and then, no one wanted to commit to daily caregiving. The local after-school program was perfect for us!"

Because school-sponsored programs are held on campus, they also can make for a fairly stress-free arrangement. It certainly eliminates the need to deal with the headache of transportation logistics. An added bonus is that your child can spend time with many of her schoolmates and experience "educational enrichment time" that is usually part of the deal. Hands-on homework help from someone else can be a huge lifesaver on days when Mom's patience is worn thin from dealing with office politics, unhappy customers or frustration from staring at a computer screen all day.

Speaking of school: If your child is in kindergarten and attends school only half a day, inquire about enrolling for two sessions. Many schools will allow you to enroll for a full day of kindergarten, although it may cost an additional fee.

But if you're up for a little more planning and your child needs a lot more excitement, check out your local YMCA or community center to see what they offer in terms of after-school programs. For some families, this is the perfect fit. One mom shared with me: "My son, Michael, was dying to play soccer, but there was no way that I could get him to the practices with my rigid work schedule. The YMCA provided a place for him to go and hang out with friends, do his homework and play in several sports clubs. It made the thought of childcare a whole lot easier for him, which made it much more manageable for me."

Although having your child transported from school to the local YMCA by a program-sponsored minibus might give you pause for concern, you may want to give it a go. If you are concerned about safety on the bus, check out the situation with other moms and the YMCA staff. Personally talk to the driver and the kids to find out what sort of atmosphere the driver maintains in route from the school to the Y. Assuming you're satisfied with the transportation arrangements, knowing your child's eyes will light up at the thought of playing sports, taking karate or cooking lessons, or participating in other fun recreational opportunities may make a community center or the local Y (or Boys & Girls Club) the perfect answer for you and your child.

One mom who chose this childcare gap option said, "What a relief this has been for both of us. I no longer have to send Samantha to school crying every other day because she has to stay in school until five o'clock. Some kids love the continuation of the same educational environment. Samantha is one of those children who thrives on variety; she needs to run and play and take a break from educational routines."

If a licensed program seems attractive to you, you can find more information by checking out the National Afterschool Association (see www.naaweb.org) or your local Childcare Resource and Referral Agency (see www.childcareaware.org).

However, if your work hours don't line up with the licensed program, or if you have a child who really needs alone time after a day of dealing with her peers at school (and we can all relate to that!), you may want to take a look at other options. Read on!

## Pool Your Resources

Carpooling with another parent can be a great way to work out transportation issues. Maybe another parent who lives near the program is willing to give your child a lift after school in exchange for your picking up her child at her home and dropping her off at school in the mornings. It can't hurt to ask. If you're willing to make the effort to access the mom network, you might find that you have more than one win-win option available to you.

## Exempt Programs

Exempt programs make up another category of after-school childcare options. Geared toward middle-schoolers and up, exempt programs are drop-in programs, which means each facility has its own set of "house rules" (unlike licensed programs that are required to conform to certain regulations), and do not require student registration. Billed as "a safe place to hang out," these programs are often housed in community centers or churches and provide general supervision for the attendees du jour.

This mom expresses a sentiment common among moms of tweens: "My seventh-grader was old enough to stay home alone, but he got lonely and bored. Having the teen center drop-in homework time was really a perfect solution for us. He would come home after school, grab a snack, then walk to the community center and hang out there until I got home." Many tweens are ready and willing to stay home alone, but as parents, we still need to have control over how long that time alone is.

Although these exempt programs are often free and usually provide a safe, supervised place where kids can hang out, do homework and play games, you really have to have an open and honest relationship with your child, and a high level of trust, for this arrangement to work well. A personal visit to the community center is highly recommended, and it is also wise for you to drop in unexpectedly now and again to observe your child, and to get to know the supervisors as well.

Meeting and interfacing with your child's teachers or after-school caregivers in a positive way is always a worthwhile investment that fosters goodwill and trust. A friend of mine said, "I always made it a point to chat with the caregivers and send thank-you notes or a plate of treats when I could. This paid off in the caregivers' feeling comfortable enough to call and let me know if they noticed that my child seemed upset or headed toward any kind of trouble. It behooves parents to make friends with and show appreciation for the people who care for their children. Caregivers who feel a parent's appreciation are apt to do their very best for that child."

If you decide that an exempt program is the way to go for you and your child, be prepared to set ground rules. For instance, if you let your child walk to a local after-school community center, make sure you always know when your child will be there (and when he'll be going home or to a friend's house). Draw up a contract between your child and yourself that outlines your agreement for after-school scheduling, including penalties for breaking the rules or changing plans without prior approval.

As an added precaution, add a line to your cell-phone plan. Many wireless providers have a family-share plan so that you can share pooled minutes for an inexpensive cost. If you are ever concerned that your preteen or teenaged child is telling you that he is one place when he is really somewhere else, you can ask your child to give his cell phone to the supervisor, parent or caregiver to confirm where he is. Check out www.fireflymobile.com for an easy-to-operate, five-key, kid-friendly cell phone.

## Don't Count Out the Library!

The local library can be a great safe place for middle-school-aged kids to spend some time after school hours. Comfy places to relax, monitored Internet access and spacious tables for doing homework provide a perfect environment for studying. Many libraries also host special after-school programs for teens who love to read.

Consider your child's personality. If she is an independent preteen who is self-motivated, does well without structured activities and enjoys quiet environments and the company of books, the library could be your best bet for filling up the gap.

## Self-Care

The question came out of the blue: "Mom, can I stay home alone?" You couldn't answer—all you could think was, *Calgon, take me away!*

In the good ole days of porch swings and friendly neighbors, our parents and grandparents probably didn't think twice about letting their kids stay home alone. In fact, in some small, trusted communities, there weren't any latchkey kids because most people never locked their doors. Alas, the times are a-changing, and not always for the better.

The phrase "latchkey kid" was coined to describe the many children who came home from school, key in hand, and let themselves into their home to stay by themselves until one of their parents returned from work. Today, in the United States alone, over 7 million kids between the ages of 5 and 14 are responsible for this type of self-care.

For a child who is mature and well prepared, staying home alone a few hours a day can actually be a great way to build self-reliance skills. For others, who need consistent adult supervision, it can be a parent's nightmare. Although only Maryland and Illinois currently have laws governing the age when a child can be left home alone, the National Safe Kids Campaign recommends that no child under age 12 be left alone. Safe Kids (check out www.safekids.org) is a great resource and can help you determine whether your child may be ready to stay home alone, as well as give you information on how to prepare your child for that stage of self-responsibility.

The cons to kids staying home alone, of course, are the lack of supervision for anything they choose to do or watch; unbridled access to the Internet, TV and phone are just some causes for concern. Thankfully, all of these can be subject to parental controls, which should definitely be put into place to help your child self-monitor wisely.

Drawing up a contract that outlines the three Rs—rules, routines and responsibilities—for staying home alone will help everyone stay on the same page. Kids who are left home alone should be instructed on how to answer the door and phone correctly (how to dial 9-1-1, when to call Mom, how to deal with unexpected visitors); on general house concerns (toilet overflowing, power outage, broken glass); on how to handle conflicts with friends or siblings (when to call Mom, what the rules are); on appropriate media usage (phone calls, computer and TV); and on fire precautions and basic safety guidelines.

Families who can use self-care in combination with other supervised care options during the week often seem to have the best success. A child being home alone occasionally can be fine, as long as he isn't home alone every day. This mom found that having her son home alone two days a week worked well for their family:

> My teenaged son had sports practice until four-thirty in the afternoon, three days a week. So on those three days, I was able to leave work a little early and pick him up. We were left with only two days when I wouldn't be home when he finished school. We came up with a plan: If he wanted to spend those two days home alone, he had to agree to call us when he got home, to follow a list of rules and to take a basic health and safety course offered by the American Red Cross. We agreed to a trial run and were amazed at how seamlessly it worked out for our family.

If you happen to have a child that is a budding gourmet cook, it can be fun for all to allow him to create a meal for the family one night a week—it gives him a chance to play "chef" and gives you a break from cooking!

Lastly, a word about chores: Every child should have a few things he needs to do on a daily basis, as part of the family unit. But be reasonable with your kid. He needs a balance of school, homework, play, rest and relaxation, and household chores. Discuss what you need from him, and what he can reasonably manage given his class load at school and a teenager's real need for rest and down time. Work toward a realistic win-win.

## In-Home Childcare (Nanny Care/ Babysitter/ Au Pair/ Relative)

If your child really needs to come home and wind down after a long day, or you need flexible care that goes long past the ending time of most traditional programs, in-home childcare may be the best option for you.

## Safety First

I can't emphasize enough the need for your child to take a First Aid or basic safety course as soon as she is old enough to do so. Check with your local hospital, fire station or community center to see if they offer training geared toward youngsters.

Here are some ways to help your child feel safe as she moves toward independence and self-care.

- Sign your child up for scouting to earn a badge that requires work toward mastering safety topics.
- Enroll your child in the American Red Cross Babysitting, Safe on My Own or Home Alone training courses (courses vary chapter to chapter, so check out your local course offerings at www.redcross.org).

If it's in your budget, in-home care can eliminate lots of the hassles that come with utilizing a childcare program. If your nanny, babysitter or relative drives (and this is a part of your childcare arrangement), you don't need to worry about how your child is going to get from school to home (as a nanny, part of my job was to provide transportation for the kids to and from where they needed to be and to go). Also, you don't have to worry about whether your work schedule will fit with a traditional program's hours of operation. If you have to work late (be sure your caregiver can and is willing to stay late before committing yourself), someone can take Sara to ballet, and feed Timmy and Nathan a nutritious dinner when their tummies are howling hungry.

"When you have two kids who have completely different school schedules and after-school activities, having a nanny was the only way I could make everyone even a little bit happy," said one working mom. You can barely keep track of your own work schedule, never mind having to memorize the schedule for your two active kids. If you want your kids to be able to take part in extracurricular activities, having an in-home provider (with a reliable car and good driving record) allows them to take part in sports, music and other recreational programs that they otherwise might have to miss out on.

Because you are the boss, you can set the hours, duties and responsibilities when looking for your caregiver. You can have your in-home provider ensure that your kids have their homework done, are fed dinner and are ready to wind down for the night by the time you get home, giving you quality time with your children that you might not otherwise enjoy. Another working mom summed it up like this: "Rushing to get my kids from after-school care, making dinner and getting everyone bathed and ready for bed was not my idea of having quality time with my kids. Having in-home help allows me to come home at the end of my day and enjoy the few hours we have left together reading books, hearing about their day, relaxing and unwinding."

Most couples who need a regular nanny pay their in-home provider for full-time hours year round. When you consider the cost of finding backup care when your child is sick, before-school care, after-school care, summer and vacation and holiday coverage, you may come out ahead of the game by paying your caregiver an annual set salary. You can also ask her to take on some household management duties while the kids are in school. Of course, to afford a nanny like this, your salary has to be fairly generous. And while nanny care isn't for everyone, more and more families are discovering that having a nanny increases the quality of life for everyone, provided the nanny is the right fit for their family.

If you are a working mother, don't automatically assume you can't afford a nanny. Check it out! It may be more within the reach of your budget than you'd assumed. Visit www.nanny.org

and view the International Nanny Association salary survey to find out the average cost of a nanny in your area.

## Piecemeal Arrangements

Although there are many different options for after-school care, there isn't always a one-size-fits-all arrangement. Many working families rely on a piecemeal approach to create their weekly childcare arrangements. They rely on limited, but regularly coordinated, scheduled help from family or friends, participation in extra-curricular activities and self-care from children who are old enough and mature enough to assume that responsibility.

If your budget is tight and you have the energy, you can coordinate your child's after-school activities each week. In fact, many a creative mom has put together a cafeteria plan of sorts that turns out to work beautifully for her child.

For this option to work, you'll need to have—in addition to a hugely organized family day planner (check out www.busybodybook.com)—family, neighbors or friends to help out with limited but regularly scheduled caregiving. Check out Megan's creative arrangement:

We solve our childcare dilemma by using a little bit of everything. Mondays and Wednesdays, my mother picks the kids up at school and keeps them at her house. Tuesdays, they both attend Scouts. Thursdays, I have a babysitter that I found at church come to our house. On Fridays, the kids get off the bus after school and my neighbor watches them. In exchange for this, I take her son, Sam, home with us for a dinner and movie night so that she and her husband can have a weekly night out themselves. It's taken a lot of work to get this system up and running, and it would make some moms crazy—but this much variety works well for us. My kids are adaptable and enjoy lots of different activities. Plus, this piecemeal system is very budget friendly, freeing up funds for our family to use for eating out or for a special vacation.

## A Voluntary Option

Think about volunteering your child for . . . volunteer work! Once a week your child may be able to volunteer at a local hospital or nursing home. When I was in junior high, I would walk to the local nursing home and play games with the elderly and help serve them dinner. I believe my experience helped make me the compassionate person I am today (check out www.breadofcompassion.com) and was a stepping-stone toward my career in caregiving.

## Making It Work

Though securing childcare that works around your child's school day and calendar is a bit trickier than you might have thought, it is my hope that a few of the options laid out in this chapter hit home as solutions that could work well for you and yours. Regardless of the arrangement you are seriously considering, there are a few key ingredients that will keep your childcare choice from backfiring and prevent you from having to clean up a last-minute childcare disaster.

- Keep a current calendar. Having a family calendar will give you a heads-up regarding any scheduling conflicts that may be looming on the horizon (check out the Busy Body Book at www.busybodybook.com).

Get out a standard planner and assign a different ink color for each family member's activities. Note school holidays, closings, half days, important school events, priority business meetings, travel commitments and any other work commitments. You'll have a clear view of any potential problems, and when you record these events a month in advance, you'll have plenty of time to prepare.

• Have backup for the backup. Think through the "What happens when" scenarios of your childcare arrangements. *What happens when my sitter calls in sick? When school closes for inclement weather? When Devon's running a low-grade temp?* And start working on your backup plan. Do you have a retired parent you can call in a pinch? How about pre-registering with a sick-care center, just in case? Keep a running list of reputable babysitters handy so that you can quickly make some calls if your backup plan goes awry.

• Have a plan in place in case transportation arrangements fall through. *What happens when Grandma is running late to pick up Sam for school? Or if Kera misses the bus?* Check with your school and childcare provider about policies and procedures that apply when your child's transportation plans fall through. Is there a local taxi service that provides emergency backup transportation for kids? Does your child know the name and number of a neighbor or two he can call if he gets stuck?

Thinking through the "what ifs" ahead of time and having a backup plan can be an enormous relief when life gets sticky and your childcare arrangements hit a bump.

## SCENE 6: TAKE 2
### In the Living Room

**Gina-Marie** (*to Donna*): You know, once Bella went to school, I thought my childcare worries would be over. But actually, they seem to have gotten worse!

**Donna:** Worse? She's in school most of the day.

**Gina-Marie** (*irritated*): Yeah! That's the problem. Most of the day. I'm having a hard time finding one steady arrangement for the window of time between when Bella's school gets out and when I get home from work.

**Donna:** What about the day-care program she went to before?

**Gina-Marie:** They don't do after-school care, only full-day programs.

**Donna:** What about her school? They must offer something.

**Gina-Marie:** Yes, they do. I signed up for the wait list there, but I also found some other interesting options. Actually, I've already found childcare for Bella for four out of five days. On Mondays, Wednesdays and Fridays, Kate, her favorite Sunday School teacher from church, is going to watch Bella. On Tuesdays, Bella has a standing play-date at Jenna's. That just leaves Thursdays. If I can find a solution to Thursdays, I may have solved my daycare dilemma. Transitioning to kindergarten is going to be enough of a change for her. I want Bella around people and environments she knows and loves during her first year at school.

**Donna:** That's great news! And I've got an idea for Thursdays. Why don't you let me spend that one afternoon a week with my darling granddaughter?

**Gina-Marie** (*smiling*): Really? I hesitated to ask, knowing you've just retired and are anxious to enjoy your new-found freedom. But you know Bella would love nothing more than to be with her Grammy every week.

**Donna:** One of the reasons I retired was to spend more time with my family. One afternoon a week would be perfect for me. I think this would be a real win-win for all of us.

**Gina-Marie** (*hugging her mom*): You're the best.

---

## What steps did Gina-Marie take to solve her childcare challenge?

- *She researched her options.* Take time to figure out what options are available for after-school childcare.

- *She did what was best for her child.* Consider your child's unique situation and temperament. Does she need one-on-one attention after being in a classroom all day? Does she need high-energy activities or low-key quiet time?

- *She utilized her resources.* Ask around and use your network. Many college students are interested in part-time work that fits around their class schedules. And although you might hesitate to ask relatives, many would love to commit to a few days a month as a way to build relationships with your child. You might explore this option by asking, "There is no obligation here at all, but I'm wondering if perhaps we might be able to work out a win-win situation with Lindsey. You've mentioned wanting to spend more time with her, and I was wondering what you'd think about taking care of her after school a few days a month?"

- *She was organized.* Explore all your options, prioritize which ones best meet your child's needs and get a schedule in place. In addition, create a backup plan for the inevitable time when your careful arrangements go temporarily awry.

**Q:** *I have been interviewing nannies for my five-year-old who is in kindergarten. I can't believe a nanny wants to be paid for a full day of childcare when she really is only on duty before and after school. Is this the norm?*

**A:** With most career or professional nannies, it comes down to paying for their availability. If working as a nanny is their full-time job, chances are, they can't really afford to find an additional position to fill the midday hours. But keep in mind that having a nanny in your employ does have its benefits. You have someone ready and available for childcare during vacations, holidays or times of illness. In addition, you can often negotiate with your caregiver to perform household-related tasks while the children are at school.

**Q:** *My babysitter transports my son to and from after-school activities. Should I be responsible for paying for the gas?*

**A:** Yes. You should reimburse your childcare provider the standard IRS mileage reimbursement rate. You can find the annual rate on www.irs.gov.

**Q:** *How important is it to have a written contract with my childcare provider?*

**A:** It is vital to have a written work agreement with anyone who provides regular care for your child, even if it's a family member. Work agreements define roles, responsibilities and expectations of each party, and when these things have been ironed out, documented and agreed to beforehand, you run into fewer problems down the road.

**Q:** *If my caregiver transports my child, does she need to have special vehicle insurance?*

**A:** If a caregiver is using your vehicle to transport your child, you should add your caregiver to your insurance policy as an additional insured driver. If a caregiver is driving her own vehicle, she must have her own insurance. In some areas, she needs to purchase additional insurance that covers her when using her vehicle for business purposes. Be sure to check with your insurance provider, since laws of coverage can vary from state to state.

**Q:** *My child attends an at-home daycare after school. I'm not comfortable with the amount of television they are allowed to watch. What is the best way to address this?*

**A:** It is completely within reason to pull your caregiver aside and share your concerns with her. In a daycare situation, it's best to set a time to talk with the provider when the kids aren't around so that you have her full attention. Or an evening phone call might work well. Thank her for providing a safe, nurturing place for your child and let her know that, though you don't mind your child watching a reasonable amount of television while in her care (then specify the time you feel is reasonable), you'd prefer if he were actively engaged playing with other children and developing his social skills. If you prefer your child watch no television at all, or are especially selective about what he watches, be sure to voice your preference.

*Q: Our neighbor often volunteers to take our child for a last-minute play-date after school, and of course my child wants to go. The problem is that I'm contracted with a caregiver and even when my son doesn't attend after-school care, I still have to pay for his slot. How can I handle this?*

**A:** Let your neighbor know how much you appreciate her invitations and thank her for thinking of your child. Try this: "The kids love play-ing together and I'm so glad we're neighbors. Can we possibly set up a play-date every few weeks or on the weekends instead, because I am stuck paying for childcare when Jamie doesn't attend his after-school program, unless I give adequate notice?" This statement con-veys your desire to keep the kids connected, your sincere gratitude to your neighbor, as well as your need to plan in advance.

*Q: My preteen thinks I don't trust her because I won't yet allow her to stay home alone after school. How can I explain to her that it's not about trust—it's about safety?*

**A:** I would say just that. "Dear, this is not so much about trusting you—it's about your safety." If you think your child may be ready to test the waters of personal responsibility, devise a plan for her to slowly earn the privilege of staying home solo. Enrolling her in a basic safety course and developing house rules are a great way to start. Little by little, allow her to stay home alone, while being checked up on by you, a trusted neighbor or a family friend. If she proves that she can be responsible, increase the amount of time she is allowed to spend alone at home. She'll be taking steps toward her independence—and you'll be making progress toward letting her learn self-care.

# SUMMER CARE, BACKUP CARE AND EVERYTHING-IN-BETWEEN CARE

SCENE 7: TAKE 1
*On the Phone at Sunrise*

**Terri** (*to her sister Laura*): I know it's early, but I need your help. Kyle was up all night with a slight fever, and I can't send him to daycare. I have a business meeting this morning that I just can't miss. Can you take him for the day?

**Laura** (*still waking up*): Uh, today is Tuesday, right? I can't—I am chaperoning a fieldtrip with Jenna's class. Did you try Mom?

**Terri** (*frustrated*): Yes, of course! There was no answer.

**Laura** (*yawning*): Oh yeah, they had their bus trip to see the fall foliage today.

**Terri** (*panicked*): Ugh, I have 30 minutes before I need to walk out this door. I am not sure what to do. Ron is on a business trip until Thursday, so I am really in a bind.

**Laura**: Did you try Lisa?

**Terri** (*sighing*): She is next on my list. Got to run.

So you've got this childcare thing down. Your two-year-old loves her nanny, your four-year-old loves his preschool and *you* love knowing that your childcare search is finally over. Right?

Well, almost. But not quite. Even the best-laid childcare plans can quickly come undone. Whether your in-home caregiver has called in sick, your four-year-old is too ill to go to preschool or your perfectly planned arrangements are ready to come to a screeching halt with summer vacation around the corner, having a backup childcare plan of action is vitally important for every working mother.

| Childcare Options | Cost | Works Best for Working Moms Who . . . |
|---|---|---|
| Family, Friend and Neighbor Care | Free and up | Have ready and willing family members and friends |
| In-Home Backup Care Options | A service fee to the agency, plus an hourly fee to the provider | Need care for mildly ill children or those who prefer to have the kids home rather than at a center or the home of someone else |
| Center-based Drop-in Childcare | An annual enrollment fee, plus a per hour provider fee | Can find alternative arrangements if there are no available slots at the drop-in center and those who can schedule days in advance when backup care is needed |
| Employer-Sponsored Care | Free to subsidized and up | Have employers that offer on- or off-site backup care for their employees |
| Summer and Vacation Camps | Varies significantly | Have children who need regular childcare when school is not in session |

# Family, Friend and Neighbor Care

If you are looking for an informal, last-minute arrangement precisely because your regular childcare arrangements have fallen through, childcare provided by a friend or family member, in your home or in theirs, may be the perfect solution for you.

Family, friend and neighbor care is inexpensive and flexible, if you have an extended network of people who support you—and who don't mind your calling at 6:30 A.M. when you're in a jam. If you are fortunate enough to be surrounded by generous family and friends, be grateful and take them up on their offer to help you out with backup childcare.

But what if you don't live near family or don't have friends who are available during the day? Be creative. Form your own support network. Talk to other moms at your office or at your church. You and the other working moms you know can create the kind of safety net that you all will need from time to time. One single working mom said, "I knew that there would be a time when the kids would be sick or the babysitter wouldn't show, and I'd have a mandatory meeting, so I got all the working moms from church together and we formed a network. We exchanged information, and everyone had six or seven names and numbers of people they could trust to call if they got into a last-minute jam."

## Easy as Pie

Make it as easy as possible for whoever steps up to the plate to provide care for your child when you're in a bind. If your child is not ill, offer your friend or family member some money to take your toddler out to lunch or on a fun adventure. If your child is going to the caregiver's house, pack a backpack with his favorite foods and toys, as well as a favorite book or video to share.

## In-Home Backup Care Options

Though you will probably have to pay for it, having backup care in your home can eliminate the fuss of getting the kids up, out and off to a new location. And on a day when your kids may have to adjust to a new caregiver, having the familiarity of being home may make that adjustment that much easier.

Yes, you'll usually have to pay an agency fee, plus an hourly fee to your provider (with agency rates that run about $30 per day and an hourly fee to a provider that runs about $10-$15 per hour). But if you use a reputable agency, you'll get an experienced and qualified person to step in and turn your chaos into calm.

"There is a local agency here in Boston that specializes in short-term and temporary care," said Carol, a working mother of three in a Boston 'burb. "It's been a real life-saver. If I know my sitter can't make it or if the preschool is closed for the day, I can schedule a temp in advance. I can even call that morning if I have a sick kid on my hands and I really need to make it into work. You pay a little more, but it's really been worth it." (A note about sick kids and new caregivers: Leaving a child, especially an ill one, with a new caregiver can often be a difficult transition. Prepare your child by letting him know that a new caregiver is coming and then give him a special activity to ease the stress of the transition. A favorite DVD [or two, or three] and/or book can often provide just enough distraction for a child to deal well with having a new childcare provider for the day.)

You can also utilize online services, such as Sittercity.com to find backup providers. But be sure to find a few sitters in your area, and screen them personally, well in advance of when you actually need them. It's also a good idea to have a few trial runs to see which providers your kids seem to mesh with best.

## Center-Based Drop-In Childcare

Having your child in a structured setting with more than one caregiver can often ease a working mother's mind. "The best thing about using a center is that you know what to expect. The worst thing about using a center is that you know what to expect," shared another working mom. "You know if your kid goes in healthy, he could come out with a cold, or that because of strict ratio guidelines that are meant to protect the kids, there may not be an opening for your child when you really need it."

It's exactly because of these children-to-provider ratio guidelines that reservations are so strongly recommended for these programs. "You have to call in as soon as it's 6:00 A.M., or you won't get through," said one mom. "But if you do get through, it can be a lifesaver."

Keep in mind that many center-based programs require pre-registration. To save time and energy, register with a center before you actually need its services and complete registration materials in advance. This will also allow you to check out the drop-in center ahead of time and, if possible, get recommendations and references from others.

If your child is unfamiliar with the institutionalized or school-type setting, she might have trouble adjusting to the new childcare center. Be sure to pack her favorite toy and snack to help her get through the day.

## Employer-Sponsored Backup Care

One fast-growing trend among employers is to offer free or subsidized backup childcare as an employee benefit. "One of the reasons I accepted my new position with my current employer was for their excellent backup childcare plan. If my nanny is sick, I just call the number provided to let them know we'll be coming. In a jiffy, my last-minute dilemma is solved," one working mom at a Boston-based law firm said.

Another added bonus is that if the backup childcare center is on site, you can stop by and have a special lunch with your child. This will give your child (and you!) something to look forward to, as well as break up the day into more manageable parts for your little one.

If your employer doesn't offer this benefit, suggest that they do. Bright Horizons (check out www.brighthorizons.com) offers a free "webinar" for employers interested in providing employer-sponsored backup childcare.

## Summer and Vacation Camps

Summers and school vacations often add a level of difficulty to finding childcare. "Not only do you have to find a program that your children like," said a working mother of twins, "but you have to find one that works with your budget and schedule."

With activities that range from overnight camping in the mountains to sports or arts and crafts at the local town recreation center, summer and vacation camps are amazingly diverse. So are their price tags. Although privately run specialty camps (running up to $10,000) can exceed the budget of most average families, many American Camp Association accredited camps cost between $75 and $300 per week, per child, for day camp and $201 to $400 per week for resident campers.[1] Church camps and nonprofit camps are often less expensive than their privately run counterparts.

If you're considering the camp option, remember that a good camp experience fosters a child's independence, self-esteem and personal growth. You can choose a camp that specializes in your child's favorite activities and select programs that teach life lessons about character, compassion and caring through communal living. On the down side, because camps only operate in the summertime or during school vacations, you probably won't be able to tour a facility and meet the staff during the off-season, although some camps take part in community fairs that showcase their offerings and programs.

To locate a reputable camp, visit the American Camp Association Find-A-Camp Database, and search their database of accredited camps (check out www.acacamps.org). You can also visit the Christian Camp and Conference Association (see www.ccca.org) to locate Christian faith-based camps. The National Camp Association also provides a free camp resource and referral service on their website, www.summercamp.org.

Still not sure the summer camp option is for you? Consider this: Once a family finds a camp that they like (and that matches their kids' interests and independence level), they often send their kids year after year. Soon their kids have formed life-long friendships, together with a trove of wonderful memories.

## Making It Work

Regardless of what option you choose for backup care, here are some key points to keep in mind:

- Find more than one backup childcare arrangement. Having a few options at the ready will make last-minute scrambling a thing of the past.

- Keep a current file of backup providers handy. Be sure to include their phone numbers and their hours of availability.

- Have extra copies of immunization records, birth certificates and up-to-date statements of good heath for each child. If you choose a center-based option, they will usually require this documentation prior to admittance. Many moms keep a to-go file handy with all the required documents photocopied and ready to take out at a moment's notice.

- Keep a list (along with extra copies) of vital family information including allergies, emergency contact information, family members' basic daily schedules, and any (and all) other information that would be helpful for someone to know when caring for your child on a backup basis. This, too, can be dropped in the to-go file.

## SCENE 7: TAKE 2
### On the Phone at Sunrise

**Terri** (*to her sister, Laura*): I know it's early, but I need your help. Kyle was up all night with a slight fever, and I can't send him to daycare. I have a business meeting this morning that I just can't miss. Can you take him for the day?

**Laura** (*still waking up*): Uh, today is Tuesday, right? I can't— I'm chaperoning a fieldtrip with Jenna's class. Did you try Mom?

**Terri** (*frustrated*): Yes, there was no answer. Thankfully, I already pre-enrolled him for a spot at the local sick-care center for just such emergencies. But I promised him I would call you first. He would much rather be at your house, of course.

**Laura** (*yawning*): Yeah, especially when he's feeling under the weather. I can't take him this morning, but I can pick him up after the fieldtrip. We should be back by two o'clock if that helps.

**Terri**: Great! You're a lifesaver. If he knows you'll be picking him up, he'll give me less of a fuss about going to the childcare center. It's the King's Kids Nursery in the church on Market Street. I'll sign you in as the pickup person for around 2:00. I'll be by your place as soon as I can. I'm going to try to move some things around and be home around four. My company is pretty good about letting me off early when the kids are sick.

**Laura**: Okay, take your time. I'll feed him dinner—see you then!

## How was Terri able to manage her morning mayhem?

- *She had a backup plan.* Do your research and know your options in advance. If you choose a daycare center, pre-register so that care is available when you need it.

- *She had a backup for the backup.* Talk with friends or family members about being a part of your backup arrangements. The more options you have, the less dependent you are on any one plan.

- *She took her child's feelings into consideration.* Especially if your child is sick, consider his comfort and feelings. Try to opt for an arrangement that will put him at ease.

- *She was familiar with her employer's policies for dealing with ill children.* Often, employers are flexible when it comes to employees with sick kids and allowing you to work occasional hours from home, leave early and make up time another day, or use sick time to care for the kids when they are ill. (Think your employer isn't this flexible? You don't know unless you ask!)

**Q:** *My daughter's best friend is going to a summer camp that isn't my favorite. Now my daughter wants to go too. Should I let her go?*

**A:** You really need to identify what you don't like about this camp. If your reason for not liking the camp is more of a personal preference rather than a safety reason, you may want to consider allowing your daughter and her friend to go together. Just think how the deal could benefit you: You'd have an instant carpool buddy at the ready—and you know that your daughter would have a great time!

**Q:** *My employer doesn't really have family-friendly policies, and when my child is sick and can't go to daycare, I need to take the day off to be home with her. How can I get my boss to stop giving me a hard time and to see that this isn't my fault?*

**A:** First, be sure you are familiar with your company's time-off policy. Next, ask if you can have a few minutes of your boss's time and explain to him that you share his dissatisfaction with your childcare options for when your child is sick. Explain to him how you are left to scramble for backup care and that you always do your best to find an alternative arrangement, but when you can't, you or your spouse must take time off to care for your child. Assure him that you do what you can while you are home (fielding work-related calls and emails) and that you always make up the time that you have to be away from the office.

**Q:** *My child is older, so I need more of a "driver" for him during the summer. How can I find a reputable person to provide transportation to and from his summer activities?*

**A:** Depending on where you live, you may want to secure the services of a livery company. Companies that transport people as a business have the proper insurance to do so. You can also check with local colleges or churches to see if there is someone interested in being a chauffeur. Regardless of how you find your driver, be sure to request a background check, a driving record check, and have a clear written contract detailing the services to be provided.

**Q:** *We've employed a nanny for our newborn. When I return to work, I want to know if it's okay to bring my child to my workplace if there is a day when my nanny is sick. How can I broach the subject with my boss?*

**A:** You'll first need to evaluate whether your work environment is safe and appropriate for a young baby. If you work with chemicals or in a place with loud machines, you'll probably want to bag the idea. Also keep in mind that having a private office is much different from sharing a workspace with a few other people. Still, if you feel that bringing your child would be safe and wouldn't interfere with the work of anyone but yourself, ask your boss how he'd feel if you brought your child to work with you on the rare occasion that your childcare arrangement falls through. Be sure to stress that this would be on extremely rare occasions, such as when your caregiver can't work because she is ill and you can't make suitable alternative arrangements.

**Q:** *We have a family member who always tells us that we should call her when we are in a childcare pinch. We've called her three times and each time she has an excuse for why she can't help. Yet, when we call someone else, she complains. Help!*

**A:** I hear your frustration. The next time she complains you didn't call her when you needed a babysitter, thank her for her offer. Then gently explain that you would love to have her help, but you have noticed that each time you really need her to babysit, it doesn't seem to work out; as a result, you've made arrangements for backup care with someone else.

*Q:* *I have a friend with a child the same age as mine, and we've agreed to be each other's emergency backup for school situations. I don't mind, but in the first three months of school, I've gotten four calls to pick up the daughter because the mother couldn't be reached. That means I have to leave work to pick up her kid. How can I let her know that this isn't acceptable?*

**A:** Sit down with your friend, and let her know that you are concerned that when there is an emergency at school, she cannot be reached. Let her know that you don't mind being the backup contact for her daughter but that the school needs to be able to contact her before they call you. Advise her that it's difficult for you to leave work at the drop of the hat and that if the pattern of emergencies continues, she'll need to add an additional backup person to her child's emergency contact information.

*Q:* *I work three days a week, and my neighbor knows this. Whenever her child is sick, she automatically assumes that I'll watch her child, just because I am home. How can I get her to stop just dropping him off?*

**A:** Setting boundaries in this type of situation is crucial. Invite your neighbor over for a cup of tea, and let her know that although you don't mind occasionally helping out, you can't be her regular backup caregiver. Let her know that you've had to change your plans too often because she has unexpectedly dropped her child off, and that although you are home two days a week, you often have your own obligations to attend to. Or let her know that you can be her backup care option once every three months (or whatever is reasonable for you), but no more than that.

# SECTION 3

## OF CRAYONS AND CAREERS

# 8

# STREAMLINING HOUSEWORK, HOME-WORK, MORNINGS AND EVENINGS

**SCENE 8: TAKE 1**
*In the Foyer*

**Danielle** (*screaming up the stairs*): Mom! Moooom! Where's my backpack?

**Mom** (*shouting back*): I don't know. Where did you leave it last?

**Danielle** (*exasperated*): I had it in the living room last night and now it's gone. I can't find it and I need it. Where did you put it?

**Mom** (*coming down the stairs*): I didn't touch it. Let me ask Dad. (*Calls to Dad.*) Jeff, did you see Danielle's backpack?

**Jeff**: No, I haven't seen it. But have either of you seen my work shoes?

**Mom**: I swear, the two of you would lose your heads if they weren't attached!

You walk into daycare, toddler Emma in tow, and you can already tell that drop-off isn't going to be smooth. In fact, you'd like to drop off the planet right about now. The teacher greets you in her robe and slippers, and just as you start to wonder about *her* mind, you remember: It's Preschool Pajama Day. When Emma realizes the mistake, the waterworks begin. A quick call to your husband yields one late-for-work daddy, but he's saved the day by bringing a pint-sized pair of PJs for Emma. "Being a hero has its price," you tell him when he starts to complain, and then you give both him and your daughter a quick kiss, a weak smile and an apologetic shrug.

On the way out the door, your stomach growls and you remember that you also forgot to eat breakfast. Being a working mom is hard enough, but these morning transitions are killers.

"I've got to get it together," you mutter to yourself, "or we're all going to fall apart."

If you are a working mom, you've probably been there—and made a similar vow not to go there again.

My goal in this chapter is to help you lay out some solid routines, spawn some organizational ideas and encourage you to plan ahead in order to avoid falling apart. I wish I could promise you that if you follow these tips, you'll never forget Pajama Day or be in such a hurry you forget to eat breakfast—but we're all human, and even the best of plans sometimes fails. Your goal is not to create a perfect life devoid of bumps and interruptions; it is to smooth out what you can, create systems that help control the chaos and then learn to go with the flow when all else fails. A little humor, a little innovation, a little creativity and, frankly, learning the skill of "letting it go and blowing it off" is a big part of being a happier, more realistic and peaceful working mom.

## Taming the Transition Times

The most trying times in your parenting life are probably the transition times: mornings, drop-offs, pickups, bedtimes—basically, any time you and your child are shifting gears and entering into a new environment. How can you help your child (not to mention you!) navigate the transition times in your day?

Remember that kids thrive on routine and structure; they like to know what's coming next in their day. They tend to find security in predictable patterns and routines. Providing a way for your child to gain an understanding of how his day will go will eliminate some of the undesirable behaviors (tantrums in younger ones, lack of listening and cooperation with the older ones) that tend to rear their ugly heads during transition times.

One effective way of helping your child visualize what his day will look like is to create a picture chart that depicts the day's activities and the order in which they will happen (think of it as a child-friendly Dayrunner). Small children are not as concerned with what time things will happen as they are with the sequence of events, so having a visual picture of what comes next will speak to your child in a way he can comprehend. For example, for a child who attends preschool and is picked up after naptime, I would make a chart that describes his day with photos of the following: a sun, breakfast food, a toothbrush, shoes, a car, a school, blocks, a sandwich, a bed, then a picture of you and your child. This type of chart can be as elaborate or as simple as you want it to be, but the concept behind it is what makes it effective.

When you are planning your child's routine, thinking through what will happen on an average day allows you to come up with many ways to simplify your day, lessen your stress and make transitions tantrum free for you and your child. Here are some of my best tips for creating a transition-friendly routine:

- Have a place for everything. Having a designated place for each child's items eliminates lots of morning chaos (and the added pre-caffeine stress) associated with last-minute search-and-rescue missions for lost shoes, homework, library books, and so on.

- Utilize a corkboard. Having a bulletin board by the front door that is used for school notices and the family schedule is a great visual reminder of what's happening and when.

- Have a specific place for morning necessities by the front door. Getting Alex in the habit of leaving his packed backpack by the front door (or wherever your point of departure from the house is) at night will eliminate frantic morning homework hunts.

- Pull out clothes for the next day the night before. Laying out Mandy's clothes the night before on the edge of her bed is one less thing to have to deal with in the morning. Then do the same for yourself—you'll save time and energy in the long run.

- Use verbal cues to wind down activities. Phrases like "You have three more minutes to finish eating" or "We are leaving for preschool in five minutes" help your child prepare for what comes next.

- Sing loud and proud. Creating songs for activities also helps kids to transition into them. Who wants to clean up? No one—until you burst into your rendition of "Clean Up, Put Away," which is personalized to include the name of every child in the room. It works with older kids, too; they'll do what you want so you *stop* singing.

- Keep goodbyes short, sweet and final. One of my pet peeves when I'm volunteering in the church nursery is the prolonged goodbye. You know the ones I'm talking about—the 15-minute goodbye that leaves Charlie screaming for Mommy, who then returns, unable to handle the tears. Sometimes the nanny in me wants to issue a time-out to Mom for making matters worse. I want to scream, "Leaving him is not an option—you are going to do it, and you know that when you peek around the corner in three minutes, he'll be fine. So stop prolonging your departure!" But instead, I put on my happy nanny face and gently escort the mommy out the door, assuring her that I will page her if for some reason her son doesn't settle in the way he has every Sunday for the past two years. Week after week, I wonder if I am starring in an episode of a new reality show, "Drama Drop-offs" or something of the sort. This is all to say that if you've chosen a caregiver or caregiving situation that you trust, and if you are determined to have your child stay there, put on your happy face, appear to be confident and, with a relaxed smile, say your "See you soon!" and get going. The transition will go much more smoothly than you think.

## Caregiver Communication

Whether you've hired a full-time nanny, your mom cares for your children or your kids attend a local preschool or daycare program, communicating with your caregiver is one skill you surely want to master. Effectively communicating with your caregiver goes a long way toward creating a positive experience for your family. From your daily greetings to your performance evaluations (whether a parent-teacher conference or a nanny review), how you interact with your child's caregiver can have an enormous impact on your child's peace of mind.

Building a solid relationship with your caregiver during the "good times" will lay the foundation. That way, you'll have a good relationship that can weather the times when things get shaky—and no matter your childcare choice, those times will come, just as they do in any relationship of value. The way you present yourself, whether warm, friendly and honest, or cold, distant and reserved, will convey volumes to your caregiver.

Since most of the day-to-day issues you will face are fairly simple and common, a journal is a great way to communicate with your caregiver. For a nanny, having a daily log handy to record meals, activities and other comments is a vital necessity. I always tell parents when I am juggling the needs of newborn twins that I'd be lost without my journal. I like to keep track of who's doing what and when so that I have a reference tool to look back on if issues arise. With twins, as you can imagine, it's doubly important to remember which child was fed and when, who took a longer nap, which one got the baby Tylenol for their fever and at what time, and so on. This is especially important when Mom and nanny are trading off the babies to each other. The more information each one has, the better care the children receive.

But journals aren't just for babysitters and nannies! Keeping a journal in your child's backpack is an easy way to facilitate two-way communication between a caregiver or teacher and parent. Attempting to talk to your child's daycare provider during drop-off time can be a challenge, and expecting her undivided attention during this hectic transition time is unrealistic. A journal is a perfect way to ask simple questions or convey basic information, at a time when things have settled down for the day. Just make sure that when the caregiver reads your note, she responds in some way to acknowledge it, and vice versa. If no action or comment is needed, the caregiver can simply put a checkmark on the note to indicate that she has read it.

When issues arise that need to be discussed in person, it is best to set a time to meet with the teacher or caregiver without your child. Addressing your provider in a non-judgmental way will go far in helping you to be heard. For example, if your concern is that Ava complains that her teacher doesn't like her, try saying something like this: "I'm not quite sure why, but for some reason Ava is feeling that you don't like her. I've seen how great you are with her, so what I am concerned about is her *perception*. What can we do to help her see that you do indeed like her?" By doing this, you share your concern in a way that facilitates problem-solving, rather than finger-pointing. Be sure to follow up with your provider once your mutual plan of action has been implemented. Later, praise your caregiver for the resulting positive changes, and thank her for taking the time to work through the issue.

In the rare case when pointing a finger may be unavoidable—and indeed appropriate—set a time to speak with the provider and provide a written statement of your concern. If the issue is serious, you may also want to make sure that a witness, such as another teacher or supervisor, is present.

Having In and Out boxes for your child is a great way to keep track of permission slips, special events, notices and all other school-related paperwork. You can use standard paper-sized office boxes in bright colors to differentiate between incoming and outgoing papers. Or you may prefer to have a vertical file hanging by the door or in the kitchen to help you quickly and conveniently manage the paper trail that finds its way home from school and back again. If you have several children, they will probably need their own In and Out boxes or files with their names on it.

## On the Home Front

"Call the plumber!" your husband yells from the basement. You begin to search through the junk drawer to find the plumber's business card from last year, when he installed the washer. You sift through the drawer and discover a dog-chewed yo-yo, pencils without erasers or points, Strawberry Shortcake stickers and a business card—from the dog walker. You sigh and think, *There's got to be a better way.*

One of the first things I do when I start a new position is to take inventory of all household-related and emergency contacts. There is nothing worse than being in a house that is not yours when the electricity goes out and you don't know which electric company provides power to the home.

Whether yours is a personalized list or a printout from my favorite home organization website www.homeconvenience.com,* having a master list of all household-related contacts is a necessity. Grab a pencil and start your list: electric company, phone company, water company, heating company, plumber, electrician, mechanic, cable company, car insurance company, home insurance company, health insurance company. Include your account number, the name of the provider and the phone number. Head to Staples (or your favorite office supply store), grab a binder and some plastic page protectors and *voilà!* Information will never be lost in Junk Drawer Purgatory again.

It is also a good idea to include in the binder profiles for each member of the family. This profile should detail vital information such as date of birth, medical conditions and phone numbers of physicians. Each profile can be as elaborate as you want it to be, listing anything and everything—from underwear sizes to ring sizes—if you are a lover of details!

Having a master family schedule is also a great way to eliminate household confusion. While on your trip to the office supply store, grab one of those oversized calendars and some colored markers (I prefer the dry-erase type). Assign each family member a color, and fill in the calendar with everyone's day-to-day schedule.

When assigning your colors, make sure you save one color to designate family time and then be sure to *include* time for family on your calendar (this is even more important as the kids get older and their activities leave everyone feeling disconnected). Once a week, try to plan something special to do as a family.

* I love this website! Click on the link for a free 30-day trial.

Whether it is going for a weekend morning walk or taking a special outing to the park, having regularly scheduled family times will ensure that the ties that bind don't unravel amid the busyness of life.

The same goes for date nights and Mommy time—make them both priorities! Having regularly scheduled times, say the first Saturday of the month for date night and the third Sunday for a few hours of alone time, will help to ensure you get the time you need to show your spouse, and yourself, affection and respect.

## Manageable Mornings

Though mornings with kids can be hectic and unpredictable, you can always count on one thing to be the same: being greeted (as you come down the stairs for your first cup of java) by a trail of misplaced homework, followed by a sea of mismatched shoes that leads to one panic-stricken child (or husband!) who can't find what he needs to start his day.

If the midweek scavenger hunts have left you searching for a more manageable morning system, take a deep breath, find a cozy seat and get ready to receive a plan of action that will leave you searching for only one thing: a second cup of coffee to enjoy as your household is transformed from chaos to calm in three easy (okay, *fairly* easy) steps: (1) Prioritize. (2) Organize. (3) Activate. These three words are the lyrics to your new mental theme song. Repeat them often, as they are the steps to success when it comes to organizing your home (and your life!) in a way that eliminates the frustrating last-minute searches for the must-haves, enabling everyone to get out the door on time.

### 1. Prioritize

For today's working mothers, learning to prioritize is critical. In case you have any doubts about that, let's do some basic math. There are 168 hours in a 7-day week. Let's say you clock an average of 50 hours of work per week. You're down to 118 hours. Subtract 8 hours of sleep a night, and you're down to 62. Take away another, say, 7 hours of time spent in the car commuting to work and childcare, and 15 hours a week of meal preparation and eating. Now you're down to a mere 40 hours. Forty hours a week to manage a house (clean, do laundry, grocery shop), run errands, supervise homework, attend kids' activities, spend time with your spouse, go to church, make calls to or visit with friends and family, and maybe—just maybe—sneak in an hour to go to the gym or to soak in a bubble bath.

Doing the math may make you long for a midday nap, but when you recalculate the numbers, you can clearly see that there is no time for snoozing (at least not until you've got your plan of action in place). You need to prioritize today.

When working with families, I have found that part of the reason they run into so much trouble completing and maintaining household organization is that they fail to prioritize the projects that they take on. Take back-to-school season, for example. You go out and shop 'til you drop, buying all your kid's new school clothes in record time and on a record budget. You get home, satisfied with your excursion, and begin to put away the new fall wardrobe. *Uh-oh*, you think to yourself as you realize that there is no place to actually store, hang or put away the new fall wardrobe. The closets and drawers are bursting with clothes that don't fit, clothes your child won't wear and even some clothes with their tags still attached.

As usual, hindsight is 20/20. You realize that organizing the current wardrobe (and taking an inventory of it before the big shopping trip) should have taken priority over purchasing new clothes.

For prioritization to have any real meaning, you need to have a clear objective. If your objective is to have a functional, usable closet, it needs to be organized. If your objective is to save money, you need to know what you already have so that you buy only what you need. If your objective is to bring home a new back-to-school wardrobe, you still need to have somewhere to put it.

Your objective could be a set of personal goals (to keep an orderly house) or a state of being (stress-free living) or even your family's personal mission statement—whether it is formal ("We put our faith and family first") or funny ("We don't believe in miracles—we *rely* on them"). The goal of prioritizing, then, becomes the means whereby you can achieve your objective with the least amount of effort, in the least amount of time. And as we've already seen, a working mom's time is limited—her hours are precious.

How exactly will you get all that needs to be done accomplished in a single day? You'll begin by setting some personal priorities that will put time on your side.

The cliché "There's so much to do and so little time" was surely coined by a working mother. One way to help prioritize household and home-management tasks is to make a daily to-do list (a simple yellow legal pad is my favorite to-do list tool). Spending five minutes a day making this list will help you save time over the long haul.

Your daily to-do list should have three columns: the "Must Do" column, the "Should Do" column and the "Would be Nice to Do" column. The "Must Do" column consists of items that need to be completed today; the "Should Do" column consists of items that need to be completed before the end of the week; and the "Would Be Nice to Do" column outlines the items that can wait until you have more free (ahem, unscheduled) time.

Once you've completed the list, keep it posted in plain view (the fridge or a kitchen corkboard work well). Delegate any items that you can delegate—maybe your spouse can stop at the pharmacy on his way home, or your daughter can walk the dog. Then check off the items as they are completed. Honestly, does anything on earth feel quite as good as checking off an item on a to-do list? (Okay, there are a few things—but not many . . . at least not for a task-oriented person like me!)

Now is also the time to consult your budget to see if you can afford to hire out any of the tasks on your to-do list. In the professional world, they call this "outsourcing." Sometimes the cost of paying for personal shopping and errand running, housekeeping and dog walking are outweighed by the time you'll have to do other, more important, things. You may be able to hire a family employee (a retiree, a college student or a single mom) who is willing to do a wide range of tasks for a set hourly rate.

You can also begin to develop some long-range planning systems. For example, you can designate every Saturday as your official laundry day. Friday evenings are pizza out and grocery-buying night. Saturday evening is date night. Sunday nights are family nights. Sunday afternoons and Tuesday evenings could be "Mom time." Having a designated day for designated tasks relieves a lot of stress. Case in point: When you pass the almost-full laundry basket, you can say to yourself, *It will get done on Saturday. I'm now going to read a book and take a bath, guilt-free.*

I hope you're realizing that you can use your many talents to make your household run as efficiently as your workplace. It's amazing how many professional skills can be adapted for home use. This is certainly one concept that working moms need to bring home, along with their paycheck.

## 2. Organize

If the thought of spending a Saturday afternoon at the Container Store is enough to make you volunteer to babysit your neighbor's three-year-old triplets (and their two dogs), I know just what you need. Stores that specialize in organizational items can make the organizationally challenged feel like an elephant in a china shop. You feel so out of place and overwhelmed that you just don't know where to start (or for that matter, how to use half of the gadgets and gizmos on display).

"Inch by inch, anything's a cinch" is the approach I take when helping working moms get used to the idea of organiza-

## Stock Up

A tip for laundry if you employ the once-a-week method: Stock up on a lot of socks and underwear; two week's worth per family member isn't unreasonable. They are inexpensive (when purchased on sale!) and don't take up much room, but oh, the angst that arises when someone runs out of them! If you or your kids wear mostly jeans or a lot of white T-shirts, stock up on these as well when they go on sale. Laundry can be pushed to one day a week, but only if you have plenty of clothes for everyone to make it through a full week without worry.

tion—creating a place for everything so that everything will have a place.

### Scheduling and Storage

Managing your own life is challenging enough, but when you throw in your kids and your spouse's schedules, even a Palm Pilot could burn out. One effective way of keeping track of who is doing what, when, is to invest in an oversized combination cork-and dry-erase board. I suggest hanging one in the kitchen by the fridge—a place even your husband can't miss. You can pick up simple inexpensive ones at your local dollar store, or you can order more elaborate, custom-sized and framed (to match your décor) boards at www.artconceptstore.com (I've used this store before and love it!). Dry-erase boards are valuable because you can jot down notes, reminders and other important information in one handy place. And unlike Post-It Notes, your notes will never get lost.

Corkboards are a necessity for every busy family because they are multi-functional. You can tack up monthly calendars, school information and reminders, and printouts of emergency numbers. Many websites offer free downloadable and printable blank calendars and phonebook templates (check out www.print-free.com). You can also hang keys on oversized push pins, jab your earrings in them when you come home from work (so that your toddler won't have to resist the urge to pull them off and eat them) and tack up coupons you normally misplace shortly after clipping them from Sunday's paper. If you don't like the cluttered look of a corkboard, try placing it in the laundry room or another room that isn't frequented by guests but where you and your family can see and access it easily.

When you are streamlining your family's calendar, a computer-generated calendar can be very handy. If you have older children or a technology-savvy family, you may enjoy using an online program to sync all your activities and events. Homeconvenience.com allows you to enter your family's scheduling information and create a customized calendar. The service will also email or text message appointment reminders and allow you to sync your family calendar with your PDA (Microsoft Outlook also has a great calendar/reminder program).

Customize your family calendar with important activities and events, holidays and school closings, childcare arrangements, after-hours work commitments and other appointments (I recommend printing out the next two months and stapling them to the schedule for the current month). Using a different-colored ink for each family member will make it easier to identify at a glance who is scheduled to do what. If you're using a computer-generated calendar, you can change the font color or even highlight important dates as needed. Once your calendar is up to date, make a few copies and tack one on your corkboard, give one to your spouse, bring one to your office and keep one in the car.

In deciding what kind of calendar to use, consider what works best with your personality and be honest with yourself about what you know you *will* do. If you are a computer person, you'll probably enjoy the tech-friendly calendars. If you are more of a hands-on writing person, go with the dry-erase version. Basically, do whatever floats your boat, as long as you've got a functional calendar system to help you know who's floating when and where (and who needs to be rescued from the sea called over-scheduling).

Be sure to implement a family-wide policy when booking commitments outside of the normal day-to-day schedule: Every member should take the time to check the family schedule before committing to additional activities and events. If someone is caught off guard without a schedule in hand, they should respond with a default answer when asked about their availability. "I'll have to get back to you" or "I need to check my schedule" will save you from having to reschedule events and appointments if you discover you're already committed.

Older kids will also benefit from having their own personal office space. Whether it's a corner table in the dining room or a spare desk alongside yours in the study, a space set aside for doing their homework will eliminate the much dreaded daily hassles associated with getting them to do their studies. Give them their own desk set, complete with pens and pencils, a computer station and their own "junk drawer" filled with some Mom-approved treats. You'll be surprised at how quickly your kids make their personal spaces their second homes.

Kids also seem to do better when they have a designated homework time. Some kids need a break to reenergize between school and homework, and others do better when they jump right in and get it out of the way. Figure out what style suits your child best, and come up with a consistent routine that everyone learns to respect.

I know I've said this before, but it's really worth repeating: In and Out boxes for each child are great for ensuring that important school or daycare notes and bulletins don't get lost in the backpack void. They are a true necessity for school-aged kids, and for moms who are too busy to chase down permission slips and progress reports that need to be signed and returned to school. Pick a colored folder for each child (if you want to be super-coordinated, pick the same color that you selected for the child's "calendar ink"), and keep the folders in an easy-to-reach place. Be sure to keep the location consistent, and encourage your children to empty their backpacks as one of the first things they do when they return home from school or daycare.

Designating a place to store lunch boxes and backpacks is another way to eliminate the last-minute search for morning necessities (remember the "have a place for everything" habit?). Hall closets and foyer cubbies work really well as storage for the things that your children need to take to school or daycare each day. For elementary school-aged children and younger, having a basket or bin in the front hallway closet is a good place to store shoes. If the closet is big enough, it can also be the storage area for their backpacks, jackets, winter accessories and lunch boxes. You can easily store hats and mittens in a basket on the closet floor or in a bag hung from a coat hanger on the closet rod. If space allows, you can install hook screws on the interior of your closet. Be sure they are strong enough to hold the weight of a schoolbag (those books and notebooks are heavy!). And don't forget that older kids can also benefit from having a designated place to store sporting gear or musical instruments.

You can also create your own bag in which to store your child's library books. On your next trip to your local craft store, purchase a canvas bag and some fabric paint, then write your child's name on the bag. Decorate it together with your child, and ask her to store her library books in her special bag (perhaps placed near her bedside table for nighttime reading) so that you aren't left frantically searching for overdue library books mixed in with her own personal collection or school textbooks.

When on the go with kids, storing a little bit of everything in the trunk of your car can be a saving grace. A change of clothes for each family member, a big beach towel (in case someone gets sick, or as a blanket in a pinch), snacks, bottled water and a roll of paper towels will come in handy. If you are the mom of younger ones, always keep two diaper bags ready to go: one in the house and one in the car.

Whenever you find yourself stressed, looking for the same thing again and again, whether it's a hairbrush, a backpack or library books, that's a signal that you need a system or that your current system needs an overhaul. Spend just a few moments asking yourself: *How could I make this easier for myself?* and *What system/container/routine might solve this hassle?* Then implement that system—you'll be so glad you did. Don't worry about organizing everything all at once; that's too daunting. Remember: inch by inch. Start with the situations that most often yield hair-pulling moments and tackle them first. Then, like me, you may find that being organized is such fun that it takes on a life of its own. To me, it's more than a hobby (actually, it's become my career!).

### Key Areas to Organize

By now you may be thinking to yourself, *My entire house needs an organizational miracle makeover!* Sit back. Breathe deeply. While it's true that most of us could use a bit of help throughout our homes, there are a few key areas where you'll get the most bang for your buck (and your time and effort).

**Bedrooms.** Kids need a quiet place to settle down at the end of a busy day. Creating an organized environment in their bedroom will help your child to unwind, whether it is for a short afternoon break or before they hit the hay. This is one room where less clutter means less distraction. If you want well-rested kids, less distraction is what they need.

Creating an organized bedroom for your child will help keep his things neat and orderly and help him develop a genuine understanding of the importance of caring for his belongings. When you tell him to pick up his clothes, he will know that you mean to throw them in the hamper, not under the bed. And when he's trying to find his favorite baseball card, he won't have to look far, because it's exactly where it was supposed to be.

Ideally, the bedroom should be a fairly toy-free zone (except for books and stuffed animals for evening "wind down" time), but that's only if you have enough room in your home for a separate playroom for the kids. If you allow your child to have toys in her room (or because of space limitations you have no other choice), be sure to have a set policy that all toys get put away before bedtime. Shelving is a great way to store toys, but if your kid's room is lacking in that department, big baskets or bins are a good alternative (Homegoods, TJ Maxx, Hobby Lobby, Ross and Marshalls are all great places to purchase oversized baskets at a reasonable price).

Having a hamper in your child's room will also promote good habits and foster independence. Be sure the hamper is child-friendly and easily accessible. Pop-up mesh hampers and laundry baskets work great for young kids and are often lightweight and easy for them to carry back and forth from the laundry room.

Placing a bin on the floor of your child's closet will give you a quick way to eliminate closet clutter. Toss in clothes that don't fit or clothes that your child just won't wear. At the end of each season, sort through the bin. Store what you need for another child down the road, and donate what you don't to a friend, family member or charitable organization that collects kids' clothing.

You can keep your kids' drawers organized by assigning a drawer for each type of clothing. Put socks and underwear in one drawer; nightwear in another; long-sleeved shirts in one and short-sleeved shirts in yet another; and pants in another. You'll have to tweak the drawer assignments based on the amount of dresser space you have. Once you get a system in place, keeping up with it is fairly easy.

Hanging clothes in the closet can make managing your child's wardrobe much easier. Hang clothes in groups, either by outfit or by item; then within each set of items, arrange by color. If you're dealing with clothes of different sizes, use a hole punch to put a hole about an inch from the top of a piece of 8.5 x 11-inch paper and then write the size on the paper. Slide a hanger through the hole and use it to divide the sizes. Regardless of what method you choose, be sure to select your child's outfit the night before and lay it out where your child can easily reach it.

When you're dealing with laundry for two or more little ones, it's easier to keep up with the volume by throwing in a daily load. But I'm a nanny whose workplace is at the home, so you may find that a twice-weekly routine works better for you. Still, you might consider using the washer as a hamper so that you don't get buried in dirty laundry. Whenever you change your baby or toddler, just toss the outfit in the washer. When it's full enough to do a load, all you have to do is add detergent and you're good to go.

**Bath Time.** Encouraging your child to have lengthy nightly soaks is all fine and dandy for moms with one child, but when you're dealing with two or more, short and sweet is your survival code. If you're lucky enough to have a home with two full bathrooms, dedicate one as strictly for kids. In the closet or in the drawers of the vanity, store jammies and diapers, wipes and bath "fixings" for young ones. Older kids may like to hang their PJs on an over-the-door hook on the bathroom door. You'll also want to put a hamper in the kids' bathroom to prevent piles of clothing from building up on the floor.

If you're limited to a shared family bathroom, give your older children their own "space" to store their soap, deodorant and any other personal-hygiene items. You can also give older kids a small tote (like the one college kids use) and have them store it in their room.

When you have older siblings, you can use a kitchen timer to keep showers short. Younger children can be bathed in a *clean* and *disinfected* kitchen sink—this is especially time-saving for mothers of multiples. Store extra PJs, body wash, shampoo and towels in an out-of-reach area in the kitchen, and when it's bath time, be sure to have everything you need handy so that you never are tempted to leave your child unattended.

**Photos.** Organizing family photos is one of those overwhelming tasks that are often on the perennial to-do list. But until you get that rainy day when you can sit and organize your scrapbook or album, consider putting your collection of photos in a few photo storage boxes (shoe boxes will work well, too). As time permits, sort through your photos, placing photos from each year into their own box and labeling each box with its year. Then sort through each box using rubber bands or envelopes to divide photos by month, or season, according to your organizational preference. Clothing, scenery and activities should help you to "guesstimate" what was taken when.

Now that you have the backlog taken care of, put a system into place for processing new photos. As you print or place orders for new photos, be sure to order an index print and a digital copy of your photos on CD. Keep a photo storage box in the kitchen and, after the photos arrive, label them and place them in the box, in the order you receive them.

Whether you're a creative "scrapper" or prefer a more classic album, decide how you want to preserve your family history. Once your photos are chronologically sorted, you'll be able to add them to the album of your choice as time permits.

Once you develop a system, it's easy to keep up with. The key is to use a system that you find easy to maintain.

## 3. Activate

So now that I've shared some of my best, most practical organizational tips, it's time to put them to use. Whenever you start a new system or routine, it takes time to adjust. You will also need to tweak each system so that it fits the specific needs of your family.

Before you implement a new system, take a little extra time to get everyone on board. For example, if your kids are now required to put their shoes in a basket in the closet, sit down with them, discuss the changes and give them some time to get used to their new routine. If they are elementary school-aged or younger, it's going to take daily prompting before they get the hang of the new way of doing things. As well, keep in mind that checklists (with pictures for pre-reading kids and words for reading kids) can help kids understand what is expected of them.

Consistency will determine how successful you will be in implementing a new routine or system. Resist the urge to give up on a new method. Give yourself a full three weeks before you rate the effectiveness of how your new routine works (remembering that it takes 21 days to change a habit). It may take some investment of time to get your plan into practice, but once your new routines are fully operational, the time and energy you will save in the long run are more than worth the short-term effort.

## SCENE 8: TAKE 2
### In the Foyer

**Danielle** (*screaming up the stairs*): Mom! Moooom! Where's my backpack?

**Mom** (*shouting back*): Remember, we put a hook on your door yesterday so that you could find it easily.

**Danielle**: Thanks! Here it is!

**Dad**: Have either of you seen my work shoes?

**Mom**: In your shoe bin, dear.

**Jeff**: What d'ya know? Honey, thanks for your efforts to make a place for everything. It won't be long before we're used to the new routines, and I can already see how our mornings are going to be less hectic and more peaceful.

## HOW DID THIS FAMILY MAKE MORNING MADNESS DISAPPEAR?

- *They had a place for everything, and everything had its place.* Having a designated place for things makes for smooth mornings and tidy evenings.

- *Everyone knew the system.* Make sure each family member knows that everyone has a special place for his or her belongings—and where that place is (but remember that it takes time to acclimate to a new routine!).

- *The whole family was on board with the system.* Ensure that everyone understands the new system and supports it.

- *The family saw value in the system.* Everyone's goal is to get out of the house on time, and most family members will be open to a plan to help them achieve their goal. If a system doesn't prove its value within a month, it may not be the right system for you.

---

**Q:** *I have one boy and one girl that I often bathe together to speed up bath time. At what age should siblings stop bathing together?*

**A:** It's really a personal parenting choice, but as soon as one of the kids expresses any hints that they are no longer comfortable, bathing together should stop. Often older siblings don't mind helping bathe younger siblings, particularly if they are the same gender. The preschool or early school-aged years are often when many parents stop bathing kids together because their natural curiosity begins to kick in. Bath time can be a great tool for teaching kids that their bodies are special and only to be touched with their permission.

*Q:* *My husband is such a picky eater. I plan out our meals in advance and do most of the cooking on the weekends, but when Wednesday comes along and I pull out chicken, my husband announces he wants steak. What can I do?*

**A:** Getting your husband involved in the meal-planning process may help this situation. Let him know your weekly plan in advance and ask him for his input. Explain that preparing meals in advance allows you precious time with your family that you wouldn't otherwise have. You could also give him the responsibility of choosing the nightly meal from the already-prepared selections—that way, he can decide what's for dinner, within reason. Then again, you can always remind him that he's welcome to do the cooking!

*Q:* *I have the kids on a great after-school schedule, but when my husband pops home from work early, the schedule goes down the drain. How can I get my husband to understand that we need to follow the schedule in order to get everything done?*

**A:** Over a nice cup of cocoa after the kids go to bed, have a little chat with your husband. Give him kudos for being an awesome and involved dad, and then share with him all the things that need to get accomplished between the time the kids return from school and bedtime. Let him know that you've tried other ways, but the most effective way has been to adhere to a structured afternoon and evening schedule. Ask him to support you in implementing the schedule, and offer ways he can help keep things on track when he comes home early.

*Q:* At what age is it realistic to expect a child to pitch in and help out around the house?

**A:** Even from an early age, all kids can help out in some capacity. Even a toddler can help pick up her toys and put them in a basket. A two- to three-year-old can make her bed (if she has an easy-to-use, lightweight comforter), put her clothes in the hamper and put her toys away. A pre-school-aged child can help put away the groceries, sort the laundry and even with some of the cooking if he is closely supervised. Six- to eight-year-olds can fold and put away laundry and take out the trash.

*Q:* How much homework should my second-grader have? It seems like we set aside a few hours each night, and he still doesn't get all his work done.

**A:** A reasonable guideline for the amount of time a child should spend on homework is 10 minutes per night, per grade level. There-fore, your first-grader should have 10 minutes of homework, your third-grader 30 minutes and your seventh-grader 70 minutes. If you find your child is not able to complete his homework within the ap-propriate amount of time, speak with your child's teacher and let her know. Be sure that you have a clear understanding of what the teacher expects, as well as any classroom-specific homework guidelines.

*Q:* My home is too big to clean in one attempt. What is the best way to keep up with the mess?

**A:** Breaking the whole into manageable parts will help you better keep up with the cleaning. First, be sure that all family members (except the little, little ones) are keeping their bedrooms clean and tidy. It should be their responsibility to make their beds, utilize their hamper and empty their trash. Assign a day of the week to a specific task, such as mopping on Mondays and dusting on Tuesdays, or to a specific area, such as bedrooms or living areas. Deep-clean the bathrooms and kitchen weekly, while wiping down the countertops on a daily basis.

*Q: We have four kids. How can I incorporate one-on-one time with each child during our bedtime routine?*

**A:** You could have the children rest in their beds and wait as you make the rounds, reading a short bedtime story to each one. Staggering bedtimes and tucking in one child at a time is another way to sneak in a few mommy moments. You could also have a short time of prayer with each child before getting all the kids together for their nightly devotional. Also, let your husband tuck in your sons one night, while you tuck in your daughters. Then switch it up so that each child gets some personal attention from both of you.

# 9

# MEALS ON WHEELS

*Dinnertime*

*Carla walks in the door after a long day of work and puts down her brief-case. Her 12-year-old daughter, Brea, has been waiting to hear Mom's key in the door.*

**Brea** (*calls from the bedroom*): I'm so glad you're home! What's for dinner? I'm starving!

**Carla** (*walks to pantry and stares, blankly*): Brea, I am so tired. Can we just do peanut butter and jelly sandwiches and call it supper?

**Brea**: Again?

**Carla**: Hey, it was *tuna* sandwiches last night!

**Brea**: Maybe I can go over to Dory's house for dinner. Her mom actually cooks.

**Carla**: Brea! I don't need that guilt trip. But I know, I know . . . I've got to come up with a better system to get supper on the table. I'm just so overwhelmed by it all, and so very tired.

Grocery shopping and meal preparation are important, but they often end up not making it onto a working mom's radar screen. More often than not, she uses up all her energy just transporting the kids to school and daycare, and then putting in her 8-to-5 at the office, only to pick up the kids and head home to an unending to-do list of household tasks. Who has time to cook?

You, like many moms, may be thinking to yourself, *Forget a nanny! Forget a housekeeper! I'm dreaming of a live-in chef!*

Now imagine how lovely it would be to come home from work and be greeted by the smell of a pot roast and root veggies simmering in a rich broth (the Crock-Pot has made that ever-so-possible, but I'm getting ahead of myself). Then you check the Week's Menu List on your fridge door and see that there's not much else you need to do to get dinner on. Cut a wedge of iceberg lettuce for each member of your family, put a dollop of bleu-cheese dressing and a sprinkle of bacon bits on top, and your side dish is done—all without a last-minute run to the grocery store. Dinner ready in minutes!

To save time on clean-up, you've got a big stash of sturdy paper plates and cups (eco-friendly ones, of course!) in the pantry. With a few adjustments to your dinner strategy, you'll have quick and easy meals at the ready that will make drive-thrus and take-out a thing of the distant past (well, for most nights anyhow).

## Prepare-Ahead Meal-Planning

I've asked a prepare-ahead meal-planning working mother of many to share some of her best tips, recipes and secrets for pushing away the dinnertime blues.

"The first thing a busy working mom needs to do is to plan her menu," my friend Becky says. "Saturday morning works well for me, right before I head to the store. I have found it easiest to have 21 revolving dinners that I can count on to be quick, easy and working-mother friendly. I set aside weekends for more complicated recipes and for experimenting with new dishes."

I know what you are asking right now: *Did Michelle ask this wonder-mom to give her the recipes for the three weeks worth of revolving meals, which she will now share with me?* You bet I did. But first, let's get to the menu- and grocery-planning.

Becky shared her strategy with me:

I get two sheets of blank paper, and on one piece of paper I write the days of the week, leaving room to write the menus underneath. Then I plan my menus for the week, pulling from my 21 Revolving Dinners List—which I keep taped to the inside of my pantry door. I also write "eat out" or "take-out" if I am not cooking that night. On the other sheet, I write down everything I need to buy to make sure I have all the ingredients on hand for the meals I've planned. Then I do a quick check around the pantry and fridge for any staples we might need and add them to the list. Then I tuck the grocery list into my purse, and tape (or use a magnet) the menus for the week on the fridge—front and center, where the family can see "what's for dinner" at a glance. For me, this has been the easiest and most doable way to keep dinner time sane, and keep food—instead of my head—in the oven.

Now, as promised, here are "Becky's Top 21 Working-Mom Dinners"—with recipes to follow at the end of the chapter!

1. Tri-Tip Dips/French Bread with Carrot Sticks
2. Chili and Cornbread
3. Oriental Chicken Salad

4. One-Bowl Italian Sausage Pasta Dish
5. Fish Tacos and Frozen Fruit Cocktail
6. Honey Nut Salmon, Mashed Sweet Potatoes and Peas
7. Chicken Fingers with Honey Mustard Dipping Sauce
8. Asian Rice Bowl
9. Oriental Flank Steak with Potato Mashers and Salad
10. Bleu Cheese Burgers with Oven Fries
11. Grilled Three-Cheese Sandwiches with Tomato Basil Soup
12. Stew and Cornbread
13. Pineapple BBQ Chicken Pizza and Salad
14. Quesadillas and Sliced Fruit
15. Shrimp Boil with Corn on the Cob
16. Mama's Roast with Lettuce Wedges
17. Fiesta Bowls
18. Skillet Scramble with Toast or Biscuits
19. Pork Loin and Apples with Sweet Potatoes and Spinach
20. Lime Chicken
21. Quick Hamburger Stroganoff

All of the above recipes can either be put in a Crock-Pot in the morning or can be prepared, cooked and ready to eat in 15-30 minutes. "I also do lots of one-bowl wonders—meals that can be served in one bowl. I love those flat-bottomed bowls that are often used for Italian pasta dishes. They're sort of a cross between a bowl and a plate, and kids like them because there's a nice edge on them—so the food doesn't scoot away!"

## General Tips for Making Cooking a Breeze

To make cooking a breeze in any busy home, try out some of these general tips that have helped working mothers make managing meals quick and easy:

- Plan to cook no more than five meals a week. Eat out or do fast food one night and then have a "cafeteria night" when you clean out the fridge and serve left-overs (if needed, you can always stretch cafeteria night with some sandwiches and soup). Another option is to do Breakfast for Dinner night, serving omelets or French toast, sausage or bacon, and fruit slices.

- Buy one deli-roasted chicken every week to two weeks if your family enjoys them. Sam's Club has excellent prices on large roasted chickens, and they are not only delicious, but also nutritious, low fat, ready to go and taste as good or better than homemade. You may even want to purchase two: one for dinner and one to use in salads, sandwiches and casseroles for the rest of the week.

- Use the Crock-Pot once a week. From simple chicken breast with veggies to savory pot roast, fresh or frozen Crock-Pot meals are effortless. To simplify life even more, you can buy packets of seasoning for Crock-Pots or frozen meals designed for a slow cooker. And now you can even buy disposable Crock-Pot liners so that your cleanup is minimal.

- Keep one frozen casserole or lasagna on hand at all times. That way, on a day when you've run out of ingredients and just don't have time to get to the store, your meal can defrost while you're at work and you can pop it in the oven when you get home.

## Salads in a Jiffy

Try to always have the fixings ready for two to three salads that your family will eat and enjoy. It's a good idea to try to serve at least one fresh, crisp side dish for most meals so that you and your family get plenty of fiber, enzymes and vitamins that come with eating "live food." A veggie or fruit salad (which can be a mixture of canned and fresh fruits) is a great way to accomplish this goal.

Here are a few of my favorite salad ideas:

- Bring back the 1950s with old-fashioned iceberg lettuce wedges served with a good bleu-cheese dressing.

- Caesar salad made with freshly chopped romaine (or pre-chopped in a bag), a sprinkle of Parmesan cheese and bottled low-fat Caesar dressing is super easy and everyone loves it—with or without croutons. Add slices or shreds of cooked chicken to make it a complete meal. And if your family enjoys the spicy flavor of buffalo wings, toss the chicken in hot sauce (Frank's Hot Sauce is a good brand) before adding it to the salad.

- Toss pre-washed baby spinach leaves with some bacon bits or a handful of chopped nuts, any kind of crumbled cheese and raisins or Craisins. Then serve with French dressing (Catalina works well, or a mixture of Catalina and Italian) that has been heated first. This slightly wilts and softens the spinach and makes it taste even better.

## Taming the Hungries

It's a good idea to limit snacks when it's close to meal time so that everyone has plenty of room for a well-balanced dinner. I have found that keeping one of the pull-out drawers in the fridge reserved for "snacks" works well, because I choose what goes in it, and the kids feel like they have some control by choosing what comes out of it. I stock it full of fresh fruits, veggies and individual cheese sticks, all of which provide just enough healthy calories to hold them over until the dinner bell rings.

But if you're looking for some quick, creative and easy alternatives, try these kid-friendly, nanny-approved snacks.

- Most kids like canned pears or peaches with cottage cheese (or flavored yogurt) with a sprinkle of cinnamon on top. Another quick fix is bananas with drained canned mandarin oranges, some pineapple chunks, and a sprinkle of coconut or almonds.

- Add a dollop of whipped cream to anything healthy, and kids will surely give it a go! Berries with whipped cream are always a favorite.

- Sprinkle sliced apples with Fruit Fresh (they'll keep in a Ziploc bag for a couple of days), and then stick them in the fridge so that you have a quick snack to grab any time.

- Add a squeeze of citrus (lemon, lime or orange) and a dollop of honey to make the perfect dressing for any cut-up fruit. You can add yogurt as well for a creamy dressing. Feeling extra fancy? Sprinkle your concoction with poppy seeds.

- Although it's a bit of work, try cutting up a fresh pineapple and storing it in a plastic container or plastic bag. This will provide you and the kids a quick, refreshing and delicious fruit snack for several days. Fresh pineapple has loads of enzymes and is one of the best fruits out there for fostering healthy digestion.

- Save leftover fruit and blend it with ice or frozen fruit, juice or milk, and a dollop of honey for delicious and healthy smoothies for the kids and the kid-in-you!

When bananas start to darken, just peel and put in a bag; then pop them in the freezer to use later in delicious and nutritious smoothies.

• Small children love "monkey juice": Just whirl milk, half a banana (or any soft fruit) and a little bit of vanilla extract in a blender until smooth.

• Serve cut-up veggies and fruits with a dip, and kids will nearly always eat them. Fruit dips can be flavored yogurts, peanut butter and honey, or chocolate syrup mixed with healthy nut butter. Besides the basic Ranch dressings, veggies are also yummy dipped in flavored hummus dips, which give your kids a nice boost of protein along with a tasty dipping sauce.

## How to Do the "Pantry Pileup"

Here are a few of the must-haves for any working mom's pantry. Buy them in bulk if at all possible and keep your pantry fully stocked with the following essentials:

• Always have essential paper products, plastic or paper cups, paper plates, paper towels or napkins, and plastic utensils on hand. It's an amazing time-saver to buy paper products—toilet paper, paper towels, Kleenex—in bulk. You can get these at Sam's Club, Costco or other bulk-discount stores. Or buy multiples with coupons when they go on sale at your favorite grocery store.

• If you have room, keep 6-12 cans of corn, tomatoes, tomato paste, your favorite soup (we like tomato and chicken noodle), beans (any kind your family likes), and cream of mushroom or chicken (for quick casseroles). It's also great to have several cans of mandarin oranges and/or pears and peaches on hand so that you can whip up quick fruit salads or dessert cobblers.

- Always have a cake or brownie mix on hand (for those times when you realize "I'm supposed to bring something for the bake sale tomorrow!").

- Keep at least three small boxes of corn muffin mix in the pantry so that you can whip up hot bread to go with soup or chili.

- Couscous and five-minute rice (or boiling bags) are wonderful time-savers and taste yummy, too (Uncle Ben's has a wonderful five-minute wild rice that tastes fabulous!).

- Keep a large bottle of thick teriyaki sauce and multiple packets of Lipton onion soup mix as staples in your pantry. As well, I use three basic seasonings for flavoring most meals: steak seasoning, Cajun seasoning (Tony's brand) and citrus seasoning blends—so consider having these on hand. Garlic powder, oregano, cumin and dill are about the only other spices I need on a regular basis.

- Keep frozen peas and spinach and frozen fruit on hand as backups for when a recipe calls for seasonal vegetables or fruit that aren't in season.

- Try to always have the following veggies on hand: white and sweet potatoes, a head or two of your favorite lettuce (or bags of lettuce blends), tomatoes (grape tomatoes are firm and sweet all year long), and an assortment of seasonal fruit.

- Buy meat when it's on sale and freeze it. Then try to alternate beef and pork with a lighter fish or chicken meal.

- Two other World Market "finds" that I've enjoyed cooking with are panko-style bread crumbs (these are light and crunchy—perfect for quick oven-fried dishes) and Thai sweet chili sauce (this adds a little heat, a little sweet and a little garlic flavor all at one time).

- If you have a big family and can afford a second fridge, keep an extra gallon of milk, a dozen eggs, butter and a loaf of bread on hand—just in case you have unexpected guests or the week turns out to be far crazier than you plan for.

- Cooking bags for your Crock-Pot or oven are not only time-savers (minimal clean up) but they also hold the juices into your meats. Ziploc bags in quart and gallon sizes are handy, and you can also buy them in bulk.

## Meals to Go and Freezer Meals

By pre-planning your week's meals using the 21 Revolving Dinners and keeping stocked up on staples, you'll find that dinnertime is much simpler than it used to be. However, there are several other creative alternatives to help you get dinner on the table with ease these days. One of the latest and greatest cooking helps to come along is the new meals-to-go concept (Google "meals to go" or "super suppers" in your area to find a store near you).

Meals-to-go services invite you to their store's kitchen, where you find easy-to-follow recipes and ingredients for 6 to 12 chef-designed entrees. You bring an ice chest to tote your meals home to the freezer, and spend a few kid-free hours cooking with a friend, eating appetizers and listening to music. Many working moms have been pleasantly surprised to discover that the price fits well within the family budget, averaging $3-$4 per serving, and that the time they save is more than worth the expense.

Even the amazing Becky has used a meals-to-go service:

I have personally used Super Suppers several times. The pros are that I could whip together several meals in about an hour's time—with no shopping or chopping or mopping. I also went with a friend, and by splitting up the meals, we each came out with 12 meals (to feed 2-3 people) for a very reasonable cost. It's also an especially great way to get a bunch of meals together for a sick friend or someone having a baby, and I found it economically feasible. The problem was that my family loved about half of the meals, but didn't like the other half. So there's definitely some trial and error involved. And you still have to come up with a side dish, though I usually just tossed together a salad to round out the meal. But when I have a deadline or am under the weather, this is my go-to helping hand! I'd suggest every working mom try it at least once just to learn from the experience. There's a lot to be said for preparing ahead and using your freezer to save time during the week.

If you like the idea of freeze-ahead meals but want to try doing it yourself, I recommend you get the book *Don't Panic—Dinner's in the Freezer: Great-Tasting Meals You Can Make Ahead* by Susie Martinez, Vanda Howell and Bonnie Garcia. These three friends put their heads together and came up with fantastic freezer-friendly recipes that anyone can make. If you happen to have a couple of coworkers who'd like to do the same thing, you could triple your freezer-friendly recipe, then pool your efforts and get three meals for the work of one!

## Cover Up

Buy a couple of lightweight washable aprons that will cover the entire front of your outfit just in case you need to start dinner before you get a chance to change clothes. Hang your aprons on hooks inside the pantry door. Trust me, you'll save a bundle on dry cleaning!

Another popular system is based on Once a Month Cooking popularized by authors Mary Beth Lagerborg and Mimi Wilson. You spend a full day cooking, but then your meals are ready to go all month long. This is also a budget-wise way to stretch your food dollar.

## Eating Out

When thinking of fast food, consider take-out that will offer your family the best nutrition for the buck. Take-and-bake pizza places, such as Papa Murphy's, offer light, tasty and healthy versions of pizza that are a big hit among families and are a good bargain. Choose a Boston Market chicken or grilled-chicken sandwiches over greasy fried chicken in a bucket. Chinese take-out can be very healthy, as long as you avoid anything fried. Opt for Subway or Quizno's sandwiches over burgers and fries. When you avoid heavy fried food or heavily sugared desserts for a month, you'll find that your body doesn't want (and can't handle) them anymore!

Because of the ever-growing portion sizes served in most restaurants, when you're in for an especially busy week, eating out might very well be your best option. One working mom said, "If I know I have a busy week, we eat out because I know we'll have enough leftovers to last another night." And the great thing is that you don't have to eat the same thing two nights in a row! The second night, you can trade entrees with another family member and have something different.

At Christmas and for their birthdays, many working moms ask for gift cards to restaurants that offer take-out or gift certificates to their local take/freeze/bake store. They are easy to give, and people love knowing that they've not only given you a special meal as a gift, but they've also lightened your load by giving you a night off!

## Dessert

A good rule of thumb for desserts for kids is this: You can have it as long as the portion is reasonable and there's some nutritional value in it! Puddings, ice cream, cobblers, fruit, oatmeal cookies and even small servings of dark chocolate (loaded with antioxidants) all have some redeeming nutritional value. Most cookies and snack cakes offer nothing but empty calories for you and your kids. If you are going to eat dessert, be sure it's doing at least a little something positive for your body.

## Cooking Together

Keep in mind that throughout the centuries, one of the best bonding activities for families has been cooking together. So enlist the help of your kids as you cook. While you chop, cut and stir, you can find out about what's going on in each other's lives. With the menu pre-planned and ingredients on hand, you won't have to use much brain power to put dinner together, and you can concentrate more on your kids and their stories of the day's events.

## Recipes to the Ready

Now, as I promised, here are the recipes for "Becky's 21 Revolving Dinners" for you to try. Remember, they are all quick and easy and offer a bit of something for everyone.

## Tri-Tip Dips

A big tri-tip roast with grill seasoning
$1/2$ cup teriyaki sauce
2 tablespoons Worcestershire sauce
$1/3$ cup barbeque sauce
1 tablespoon of fresh chopped garlic
1 cup water

Marinate the tri-tip roast overnight in the teriyaki sauce, Worcestershire sauce, barbeque sauce, garlic and water in a cooking bag. Cook at 300 degrees for 3 hours in a cooking bag, or all day in a slow cooker.

When cooked, slice tri-tip across the grain. Heat up pan drippings to make an au jus sauce (add water if needed to thin).

Serve meat over buttered, toasted garlic bread or sub rolls, with a little bowl of au jus sauce for dipping.

## Quick Chili

1 pound ground beef, sautéed and seasoned to taste with steak
   seasoning, Cajun seasoning and cumin
1 16-ounce can of ranch-style beans
1 16-ounce can of pork 'n' beans
1 15-ounce can tomatoes with juice (blend in a food processor if
   your family prefers not to have big chunks of tomato)
$1/4$ cup catsup
$1/4$ cup picante sauce
1 tablespoon brown sugar

Cook ground beef; drain excess fat and then add the rest of the ingredients. Simmer together and adjust seasonings to taste. Serve with Jiffy cornbread muffins, and dinner's done!

## Oriental Chicken Salad

Chopped lettuce
1 cup torn or chopped store-bought rotisserie chicken

1 large can mandarin oranges, drained
Chopped almonds or other nuts
Chinese noodles

*Dressing:*
$1/4$ cup teriyaki sauce
$1/4$ cup Italian or red-wine vinegar dressing

In a bowl, layer the lettuce, chicken, oranges, almonds and Chinese noodles. Toss with dressing, or serve dressing on the side.

## One-Bowl Italian Sausage Pasta Dish
1 1-pound package of your favorite pasta
1 package link Polish-style sausage
1 32-ounce jar of spaghetti sauce
Grated mozzarella or Parmesan cheese

Boil any type of pasta your family enjoys! Then sauté until brown one package of link Polish style sausage (you can use turkey or beef or a mixture of both). Mix with your favorite bottled red spaghetti sauce and serve over noodles. Sprinkle with mozzarella or grated Parmesan. Serve with a salad, and dinner's done!

## Fish Tacos
Tilapia filets
Cajun seasoning
Olive oil
Corn tortillas
Shredded cabbage

*Special Sauce:*
Catalina dressing
Ranch dressing
Picante sauce

*Mango Salsa:*
Mango (or a few peaches)
1 tablespoon red or green onion
Cilantro
Salt
Lime juice

Season and sauté tilapia filets with Cajun seasoning (or any of your preferred seasoning salts) in a bit of olive oil. Serve in warmed, softened corn tortillas with shredded cabbage, special sauce and mango salsa.

Special sauce: Mix $1/3$ part Catalina dressing, $1/3$ part Ranch dressing and $1/3$ part picante sauce together.

Mango salsa: Chop a mango (or a couple of firm peaches) with 1 tablespoon of red or green onion and cilantro (if you like it). Sprinkle with a little salt and fresh lime juice.

## Honey Nut Salmon
2 pounds of salmon, cut into small pieces
Teriyaki sauce (to taste)
Crushed nuts or sesame seeds

Roll salmon pieces in thick teriyaki sauce, then in crushed nuts or sesame seeds. Bake in a preheated 350-degree oven until fish flakes easily with a fork. Check every 10 minutes, and then every 5 minutes until the fish is fork tender. Serve with mashed sweet potatoes and peas.

## Chicken Fingers with Honey Mustard Dipping Sauce
Chicken tenders
Mayonnaise
Rice Crispy cereal or panko bread crumbs
Seasoned salt

*Dipping Sauce:*
Honey
Mustard

Roll chicken tenders in mayonnaise, then in crushed Rice Crispy cereal or panko bread crumbs. Sprinkle with your favorite seasoned salt. Bake on lightly oiled cookie sheet at 350 degrees until juices run clear. Dip in sauce.

## Asian Rice Bowl
Cooked rice
Olive oil
Leftover chicken, beef or pork
Assorted chopped vegetables
$1/4$ cup teriyaki sauce
$1/4$ cup orange juice
Salt and pepper to taste
Thai chili sauce or red pepper flakes
Chopped nuts or fried noodles

Cook up a batch of 5-minute rice or prepare a rice bag according to directions. In a skillet, sauté in olive oil leftover chicken (or rotisserie chicken), bits of beef or pork, together with any veggies you have on hand to make a stir-fry. When meat is heated and veggies are tender, add teriyaki sauce and orange juice. Add salt and pepper if needed. May also add Thai chili sauce or red pepper flakes for extra heat if you prefer. Ladle meat and veggie stir-fry over bowls of rice, and let kids top with chopped nuts or fried noodles.

## Oriental Flank Steak with Potato Mashers and Salad
Flank steak
Citrus seasoning
$1/2$ cup teriyaki sauce

$1/2$ cup pineapple or orange juice
1 clove of garlic or 1 teaspoon of garlic powder

In the morning before work, sprinkle flank steak with citrus seasoning, and then put in a Ziploc bag with teriyaki sauce, pineapple or orange juice, garlic clove or garlic powder.

When you get home, grill or pan-fry steak on both sides for a few minutes until desired doneness (we like ours pink in the middle). Cover with a piece of foil, and let sit for a minute for juices to redistribute. Cut across the grain in thin slices.

Serve with mashed potatoes and salad. (For quick mashed potatoes, microwave a couple of potatoes until soft, and then smash them with the skin on, along with butter, some milk and salt and pepper. You can add cheese and sour cream if you are feeling ambitious.)

## Bleu Cheese Burgers with Oven Fries
1 pound ground hamburger
$1/4$ cup crumbled bleu cheese
1 teaspoon steak seasoning
BBQ sauce

*Oven Fries:*
Potatoes
Cajun seasoning
Catsup, Ranch dressing or BBQ sauce

Mix hamburger with blue cheese and steak seasoning. Grill or pan-fry. Serve with or without a bun. Delicious with BBQ sauce on top.

To make oven fries, slice potatoes (with peel on) into thin rounds. Put on a well-oiled baking sheet and sprinkle with Cajun seasoning. Flip potato rounds over about halfway through cooking time (about 10-15 minutes). Bake at 400 degrees until tender. Serve with catsup, Ranch dressing or BBQ sauce.

## Grilled Three-Cheese Sandwiches with Tomato Basil Soup
American, Parmesan and mozzarella cheeses
Loaf of sliced bread

*Tomato Basil Soup:*
1 can Campbell's tomato soup
1 16-ounce can diced tomatoes with basil
$1/4$ cup sour cream or heavy cream

For the sandwiches, use any three kinds of cheese you have on hand to create a fancier version of the typical grilled cheese sandwich. Our favorites are American, Parmesan and mozzarella combined, but any combination will work!

For the soup, blend Campbell's tomato soup with diced tomatoes with basil. Add sour cream or heavy cream as you heat.

## Stew and Cornbread
1 to 2 pounds ground stew meat
1 package Lipton onion soup mix
1 16-ounce can crushed tomatoes
3 cups water
$1/2$ cup sweet teriyaki sauce
2 potatoes
2 carrots
1 bag frozen peas
1 15-ounce can of corn
Seasoning salt

Put the meat, soup mix, tomatoes, water and teriyaki sauce in a Crock-Pot before you leave for work, and allow the stew to slow cook all day.

When you get home, microwave potatoes and carrots, chop up and add to stew. Also add a handful of frozen peas and can of corn. Taste to see if you need to add seasoning salt. Add more water if the stew is too thick. Serve with Jiffy corn muffins.

## Pineapple BBQ Chicken Pizza

1 Boboli pizza crust
1/3 cup BBQ sauce
1/3 cup spaghetti sauce
Olive oil
Roasted chicken breast, torn up into pieces
Fresh or canned pineapple chunks
Red or green onion, sliced
Mozzarella and Parmesan cheese

Mix up BBQ sauce with spaghetti sauce. Put a little olive oil on a pizza pan or cookie sheet, and heat it up in a 400-degree oven. This gives the pizza a wonderful crispy crust.

While the pan is heating up, build your pizza by layering the chicken, pineapple, onion and cheese (you can also add black olives, leftover bits of bacon or sausage, roasted garlic or jalapeño slices).

Put pizza on the hot baking sheet and cook at 400 degrees until the bottom is nicely browned. If the top needs more melting time, switch the oven to broil until the cheese is bubbly.

Serve with a salad, and dinner's done.

## Quesadillas with Sliced Fruit

Flour tortillas
Cheese
Beef, chicken or shrimp
Chopped veggies
Picante sauce
Olive oil
Butter
Sour cream or Ranch dressing

Sprinkle cheese, meat, veggies and a little bottled picante sauce between two flour tortillas. Heat quesadilla in a small mixture of oil and butter in a large hot skillet until brown and crisp and cheese melts. Cut into quarters and dip in sour cream, Ranch dressing or more picante sauce, and keep them coming until the family is full!

Serve with sliced fruit.

## Shrimp Boil with Corn on the Cob
1 2-pound bag Easy-Peel Shrimp
Cajun seasoning
Steak seasoning
2 potatoes, sliced
Corn on the cob
Catsup

Shrimp is a wonderful quick meat that can be cooked from a frozen state in no time at all. To put together a fun family "shrimp boil," get a pot of hot water boiling. Season it generously with Cajun and steak seasoning. Toss in potatoes and corn on the cob. Then, just before the potatoes and corn on the cob are done cooking, throw in a big bag of easy-peel shrimp.

Drain the shrimp mix in a colander. Serve the meal on paper plates that have been set on a table covered with newspaper (to catch the shrimp peels), along with some deli coleslaw and a big bottle of catsup.

For fun, serve with baked hush puppies, put on some Cajun music and roll up your sleeves—you'll feel like you are in Louisiana!

## Mama's Roast with Lettuce Wedges
1 2 to 3-pound chuck roast
1 envelope Lipton onion soup
1 1/2 cups water

1 can nonfat cream of mushroom soup
1 can mushrooms (optional)
Chopped root veggies
Seasoning salt
Italian dressing

*Lettuce Wedges:*
1 head iceberg lettuce
$1/4$ cup crumbled blue cheese
1 cup Ranch dressing

In a Crock-Pot, put roast, onion soup, water, can of soup and mushrooms (if desired). Let simmer all day.

As soon as you get home, toss chopped root veggies in a mixture of seasoning salt and Italian dressing. Spread on baking sheet and roast at 375 degrees for about 20 minutes or until tender.

Serve with lettuce wedges: Mix bleu cheese with Ranch dressing; serve over iceberg lettuce wedges.

## Fiesta Bowls
Corn or tortilla chips
Seasoned ground beef (or leftover chili or chicken)
Sour cream
Picante sauce
Cheddar cheese
Green onions or green pepper

Crumble corn or tortilla chips in bottom of bowl. Ladle on meat, sour cream, picante sauce, cheddar cheese and green onions or pepper. Alternative: This is even good with leftover meat spaghetti sauce.

## Skillet Scramble with Toast or Biscuits
Frozen hash browns
$1/2$ pound good quality sausage (Jimmy Dean is great)

1 dozen whisked eggs
Milk
Cheese
Chopped red peppers, tomatoes or green onions
Toast or biscuits
Fresh orange halves

Sauté hash browns and sausage. Pour thoroughly whisked eggs with a little milk over the hash browns and sausage. When eggs are mostly set, sprinkle the mixture with a little cheese and chopped red peppers, tomatoes or green onions.

Serve with toast or biscuits and fresh orange halves.

## Pork Loin and Apples with Sweet Potatoes and Spinach

1 pork loin
Seasoning salt
Brown sugar
Olive oil
Butter
2 large, peeled apples
1 cup water (or apple or orange juice)
Sweet potatoes
Spinach

Rub a pork loin (about 2 inches in diameter) with seasoned salt and brown sugar. Brown on high heat in a mixture of olive oil and butter. When browned on all sides, put the pork loin in a baking pan, cover lightly with foil and bake at 350 degrees for about 30 minutes per pound or until the internal temperature reaches 160 degrees. Meanwhile, cut apples into the pan drippings, add water (or apple or orange juice) and simmer until tender. Pour apple mixture over the top.

Serve with sweet potatoes and spinach sides.

## Lime Chicken
1 to 2 pounds of chicken tenders
Citrus seasoning
1 cup margarita mix
Cheese
Cooked rice
Crush tortilla chips
Chopped tomatoes
Chopped green onions
Sour cream or guacamole

Before work, sprinkle chicken tenders with citrus seasoning and then marinate in margarita mix (in a plastic bag). When you get home, grill or pan-fry the chicken. Put in an oblong pan and sprinkle chicken with cheese. Serve over rice and top all with any pan drippings, crushed tortilla chips, chopped tomatoes, chopped green onions, and a dollop of sour cream or prepared guacamole.

## Quick Hamburger Stroganoff
1 pound ground hamburger
1 bag wide egg noodles
1 chopped onion
1 cup mushrooms (fresh or canned)
Steak seasoning
1 can cream of mushroom soup
$1/2$ cup water
1 cup sour cream
Parsley

Boil water and cook wide egg noodles until just tender and soft. In the meantime, brown hamburger with onion and mushrooms. Drain any grease and then lightly season hamburger with steak seasoning. Add cream of mushroom soup and water. Heat and stir. Just before serving, stir in sour cream. Garnish with parsley. Serve over hot noodles.

# Making It Work

I hope this chapter inspires you to take charge of dinnertime, ahead of time. Remember, a few minutes of pre-thinking and preparation can save you not only time and frustration in the kitchen, but also lots of money. With a well-stocked pantry and good menu plan, your own home can be the best source of fast food—the kind that is nutritious and tastes great. *Bon appetit!*

SCENE 9: TAKE 2
## Dinnertime

*Carla walks in the door after a long day of work and puts down her brief-case. Her 12-year-old daughter, Brea, has been waiting to hear Mom's key in the door.*

**Brea** (*calls from the bedroom*): I'm so glad you're home! What's for dinner? I'm starving!

**Carla**: Did you check the menu on the front of the fridge?

**Brea**: Yum—fish tacos! Can I chop up the mango and make fruit salsa?

**Carla** (*tying on her apron over her business suit*): That would be wonderful. This tilapia only takes a minute to cook. I'll get the skillet hot right now.

**Brea**: And it smells so good! I love the suppers you've been making lately.

**Carla**: Well, honey, I finally put together a little menu plan, and it is really working. Should we use paper plates tonight?

**Brea**: That's a great idea. I'd love to skip dishes because I've got lots of homework.

**Carla**: No big deal then. We'll eat and toss the plates in the trash tonight. Would you look at this? All we have to do is make the sauce, and we've got dinner done!

**Brea**: And it's better than those fast-food fish tacos, any day! Why don't you change into comfy clothes, and I'll make the sauce. The recipe looks easy.

## WHAT MADE DINNERTIME A SUCCESS RATHER THAN A STRESS?

- *Mom had a menu plan.* When you plan ahead, stock your pantry and prepare in advance, dinner can be a snap!

- *Carla wasn't afraid to ask for help.* Enlist the help of your spouse and children and enjoy time spent together.

- *Because it was going to be a busy evening, Carla decided to simplify the cleanup routine.* Use the convenience of paper plates to cut down on the after-dinner mess.

- *Carla felt good, knowing she was making something easy, delicious and good for her and Brea.* Choose nutritious recipes that can be prepared ahead of time. You'll feel confident that your family is getting the fuel they need to succeed!

**Q:** *We can't ever seem to get out of the house on time. What are some easy grab-and-go breakfast ideas for my kids?*

**A:** Toast with melted cheese, bagels and cream cheese, homemade corn muffins, fresh cut fruit, cheese slices and breakfast bars are all great quick and nutritious breakfast options.

Try out this recipe for great and tasty homemade granola bars:

## Granola Bars

3 1/2 cups oats (quick or regular), toasted
1 cup nuts
1 cup raisins
2/3 cup butter or margarine, melted
1/2 cup packed brown sugar
1/3 cup honey, corn syrup or molasses
1/2 teaspoon salt
1/2 teaspoon vanilla

Toast oats by spreading on a cookie sheet or large baking pan. Bake at 350 degrees for 15-20 minutes until lightly browned. Mix all ingredients together in a large bowl with a wooden spoon. Press into well-greased 15x10-inch jelly roll pan. Bake at 350 degrees for 12-15 minutes. Cut into bars when cool.

**Q:** *My kids won't eat vegetables. How can I incorporate them into their meals without my kids catching on?*

**A:** Shredded veggies work really well in sauces, meatloaf and anything else that will hide them. But if you're not into tricking your kids, offering veggies in a kid-friendly way may peak their interest: Providing dips with fresh veggies; presenting vegetables in a creative way, such as building smiley faces or ant logs made from celery, cream cheese and raisins; and growing your own veggie garden can all make vegetables more appealing to your kids.

**Q:** *When I was growing up, my mom used to say, "Hey, this ain't a restaurant." She insisted that we eat what was served. But sometimes it's quicker to be a short-order cook and whip up something else for the uncooperative family member of the night. Is this a good idea?*

**A:** I think that being a short-order cook in addition to working, managing a home and raising kids is way too much for any mother to take on. I usually advise parents to incorporate into each meal one thing that they know each person will eat; that way they have a naturally built-in failsafe. For example, if you're serving baked scrod and you're not sure if your preschooler will eat it, be sure you also have a "safe" side dish like mashed potatoes, mixed veggies, or mac and cheese. Another way to deal with this dilemma is to allow the child who doesn't want dinner to have a sandwich—that way you aren't whipping up a whole new meal and the child's choice will still be limited.

**Q:** *Eating at our house is a three-hour event. I work so hard to prepare quick and easy meals, and then we spend a good hour and a half waiting for the kids to finish up. How can I speed up dinnertime?*

**A:** First, be sure that you are offering your kids the proper proportions. Kidshealth.org has a great guide that breaks down how much kids should be eating based on their gender and age. You'll also want to be sure that they are not distracted during dinnertime. Toys and television should be a no-no at the dinner table. If your kids are really just slow pokes, you can set a timer. Thirty minutes should be ample time for a child to eat his meal. A two-year-old can be expected to sit for about 10 minutes at the dinner table; a four-year-old, 20 minutes.

*Q:* *I've heard mixed messages about the safety of microwaving food in plastic containers. Is it dangerous to use plastic in microwave ovens?*

**A:** According to the FDA, although some substances used to make plastics can leak into foods during microwaving, the amount of leakage is well within the accepted safety margins. The FDA takes the type of chemical and the amount of leakage into consideration when regulating plastics that are used for microwaving. However, the American Plastics Council urges that you always use only containers that are meant to be used in the microwave oven. Carry out containers from restaurants, butter tub containers and other containers meant for one-time use should not be used in the microwave. Also, when using plastic wrap in the microwave, make sure that it doesn't touch your food.

*Q:* *I've heard that the way you cook vegetables can affect the quality of their nutrients. Is that true?*

**A:** Steaming, roasting and stir-frying vegetables are the best ways to maintain the vitamins, minerals and colors of fresh veggies. In other words, the less water, the better. Otherwise, the veggie's nutrients go into the water and down the drain—unless you are using the water as stock for veggie soup!

*Q:* *Growing up, we always had dessert after dinner. I remember this as a special family time and want to continue the tradition with my family. What are some healthy dessert options for my family?*

Just remember, everything in moderation! Although most families can't resist having fresh-baked cookies and cakes on occasion, consider healthy alternatives if you'd like to serve dessert on a regular basis. Fresh fruit topped with whipped cream, dark chocolate, fresh puddings and frozen yogurt are all great alternatives to processed and pre-packaged desserts.

# SINGLE MOM, DOUBLE DUTY

## *Parent-Teacher Conference*

**Mrs. Haskins** (*to Kathy, the mother of her student Isaac*): I've asked you to come in today because I am concerned with Isaac's attendance record.

**Kathy:** Yes, we've been having some trouble getting things together in the morning.

**Mrs. Haskins:** Are you aware that he's been absent 4 times this semester, late 18 out of the last 60 days of school, and 7 times been the last student on the school grounds—an hour after the closing bell rang, and the vice principal was unable to reach you?

**Kathy:** I'm sorry. I didn't realize that we'd had so many bad days, but I'm doing the best I can.

**Mrs. Haskins** (*curtly, clearly unimpressed with Kathy's response*): Kathy, I'm not sure you understand the severity of the situation. If this continues, Isaac will be in jeopardy of not being promoted to the sixth grade. He's reached the maximum of tardy days permitted per school year, and we are barely halfway through the second term.

**Kathy** (*upset and attempting to hold back tears*): I need to work two jobs to make ends meet. I deliver the morning paper before school, and if I'm running late, Isaac ends up being late. Then I waitress during the day, and my shift ends when the school bell rings. I get here as soon as I can—and the day I was *really* late, my car died. I had to catch a ride just to get here.

**Mrs. Haskins:** I'm sorry, Kathy, but I'm not sure what to say except that you need to get Isaac here on time and be on time for pick-up. I don't care how you do it—just do it. I'd hate to see such a bright and cheerful kid held back for something like too many tardies.

If you're a single working mom, the above scenario may have hit a bit too close to home. It's the "I'm doing my best, but it still isn't enough" syndrome that echoes in the hearts and minds of the mothers of nearly 10 million children in the United States.

For a sizeable number of families in the United States, working mothers head the household alone. In 2000, a staggering 9.68 million children were being raised by single mothers[1]; and according to the U.S. Labor Force, 72 percent of families maintained by single women with children ages 18 and under are currently in the workforce.[2] Consider, too, that a recent study conducted by the Center for Women and Work at Rutgers University reports, "The poverty rate for single working mother households is 21 percent, more than double the rate of families maintained by men with children and four times the rate of married couple families with children."[3]

A single mother is faced with nearly insurmountable challenges. To provide the bare essentials for her family, she often ends up working two or three part-time jobs so that her schedule works around that of her children's. Often these positions don't include health insurance or other benefits such as paid sick leave, personal days or vacation time.

Even working full time at one job a bit above minimum wage,[4] some single working mothers barely earn $12,400 per year—still well below the U.S. poverty line for a family of two.[5]

What these facts and figures mean is that a good number of single working mothers are barely making ends meet—and it's not for a lack of trying.

## Resources to the Ready!

In an age of technology, the Internet is a great way to research available resources for single working moms. In addition to the well-known federal aid services such as welfare, food stamps, Medicaid and child support enforcement, there are other financial resources that are less well known. With a bit of time, Internet access and persistence, you may be surprised to learn about the assistance that you may qualify for—and the money-saving tips that you can use to stretch your dollar. (Speaking of making your dollar go further, check out www.thedollarstretcher.com. It's a potpourri of money-saving ideas—definitely a fun website to peruse.)

Many resources available for single moms vary from state to state and have different financial guidelines that determine eligibility. And just because you may not qualify for one doesn't mean you may not qualify for another.

In addition to accessing federal and state aid, consider the merits of starting a savings account and having a budget. Knowing what you have and where it goes is the key to successfully navigating the financial world of single parenthood. There are many free Web-based programs (see www.budgettracker.com) as well as software (Microsoft Money, for example) that allow you to track your income and expenses. Having a clear picture of where you stand financially will help you to analyze your budget and identify where you need to pinch pennies.

But saving a few dollars here and there doesn't have to hurt. Here are a few areas where you can save money painlessly.

## Healthcare Help

Of the many financial burdens that single mothers face, the rising cost of healthcare is often one of the heaviest. Many single working mothers are caught in the insurance gap: Their employers do not provide health insurance, but they earn too much money to qualify for a local or state insurance program. At the same time, they do not earn enough to cover the cost of enrollment in a private health insurance plan. If you are currently uninsured, check with your local health department. Many health departments offer free immunizations and vaccinations and can direct you to free or low-cost health clinics that provide care to the uninsured.

Pharmaceutical companies often offer programs that aid eligible candidates with free medications. Check out RX Assist (www.rxassist.org), which has a comprehensive database to search for patient-assistance programs. The Partnership for Prescription Assistance (www.pparx.org) is just one of the organizations that provide pharmaceutical assistance. In addition, don't be ashamed to tell your doctor that your financial situation is tight, as they are often aware of the least expensive places to get prescriptions and may even have free samples of what you need on hand!

Many people find significant long-term savings by ordering prescriptions via mail. In most cases, mail-order prescriptions allow you to order a 90-day supply (and it's often cheaper to purchase in bulk) for maintenance medications. Also, discount warehouses like Costco and chain superstores such as Wal-Mart often offer the best prices for prescriptions.

When it comes to dental care, many dentists offer discounted rates for uninsured patients, but won't necessarily offer the cheaper rate unless you ask. Most dental schools also provide services for reduced rates. Treatments are usually done by dentists in training who are supervised closely by their licensed dental instructors.

Also, remember to shop smart. If you're on your own looking for insurance, one of the easiest ways to compare and get insurance quickly is to use www.esurance.com.

## Pampering for Pennies

Often a single mom puts her own beauty and wardrobe on the bottom of her priority list. But if a mother looks great, she will feel better, her kids will be happier because she is, and a well-groomed and well-tailored employee usually gets noticed and can more easily climb the corporate ladder. Perhaps you've seen those incredible makeover shows where, in 30 minutes of viewing time, you watch a woman get transformed into a whole new persona with the help of wardrobe consultants, hairstylists and makeup pros. Often the women are harried single moms who need a boost in both their self-esteem and their career. I wish every single mom in America could benefit from such a pampering treat, don't you?

Until my dreams come true, here are some tips for pulling together your own makeover with little or no money:

1. Beauty schools and vocational high schools provide quality services at discounted prices. The downside is that sometimes the service takes a bit longer, but the upside is that the quality is usually superb. Because students are performing for a grade and the instructor is providing training under his or her license, the incentive to turn out the best product possible is a great motivator.

2. Have a Girlfriend Makeover Party. Invite someone you know who has a real knack for makeup application to show you and your friends her best tips. (Or host a Mary Kay party so that you can get great tips and free makeup, not to mention some girlfriend socializing fun time.) Do you know a benevolent hairdresser who would give a few tips on hairstyles and coloring? Would she consider offering discounts for single moms on a budget?

3. Go bargain shopping for clothes with a friend who knows how to get fabulous style on a garage-sale budget. Look through your wardrobe and get rid of what you don't use. Then have a stylish friend take a look at your wardrobe with a fresh pair of eyes. She may put together outfits you'd never thought of matching up.

4. Accessorize! Sometimes all you really need is a new pair of earrings (check out jewels4god.org), a scarf or a pretty pendant to take an outfit from blah to beautiful! An ordinary black dress can be transformed into a show-stopping ensemble with big costume turquoise earrings or a brilliant red scarf. Inexpensive accessories are some of the easiest ways to punch up an existing wardrobe.

5. A pair of shoes and a purse in a bronze shade will go with any color outfit and work just as well with jeans as they do with business attire.

6. Have a manicure/pedicure night! One night a week, give yourself a budget-trimming manicure and pedicure. With a little practice, you can do your own

French nails like a pro. (Or engage your daughter to help and call it Mom/Daughter Spa Night. You'll get quality time with her and also get a beauty "task" out of the way at the same time.)

7. Primp up those pearly whites! One of the easiest and least expensive ways to beautify your face is to use whitening strips to brighten teeth.

## Cutting the Cost of Childcare

Of course, the cost of childcare is the heaviest financial burden that single working mothers face. Some daycare programs participate in a sliding-scale fee program that is subsidized by the state to help alleviate the financial strain for income-eligible families. Also, be sure to thank Uncle Sam and take advantage of the tax credits allowed for childcare. If you work part time, connecting with another single mother who works an opposite shift may remedy your childcare dilemma. Trading childcare—even if only on a backup basis—is a viable solution for many single mothers. Or consider taking part in a nanny share: a few families that live in the same community share a childcare provider—this can also be a cost effective way to secure quality, flexible childcare (for more information, review section two of this book, which is completely dedicated to breaking down your childcare choices and guiding you to the right fit for your family).

## A Free Education Comes with a Cost!

The costs that come along with sending your child to school, even public school, can be quite high. School clothes and supplies can make a significant cut into any family's September budget. Be sure to shop the sales, buy during off-season and take advantage of hand-me-downs and consignment shops. Calculate the savings to be had with these cost-saving tips!

- When notebook paper is on sale for 25 cents a bundle, buy enough to last all year long. Same goes with dual-pocket folders and other school supplies.

- Check out eBay—this can be a great resource for quality, inexpensive kids' clothes.

- Craigslist.org is also a great classified site that is organized according to geographic area and searchable categories. And if you enjoy garage sales or shopping at discount or consignment shops, you can find some amazing bargains.

- Although you have to take time to pick and be choosy, Goodwill, Salvation Army or Habitat for Humanity outlets can yield some incredible finds.

- Start a "Hand Me Down Rose" club with the ladies at your church or place of employment: Everyone brings good clothing their kids have outgrown to pass around and share! Do this twice a year, for summer/spring and fall/winter. You keep your closets paired down and everyone benefits.

- Collect from clearance stores. Whenever you are in a store such as Ross, TJ Maxx or Kohl's—or an outlet mall—always take a moment to browse the deeply discounted racks. Buy off-season, good quality clothes marked down to 80 percent off, and you'll be able to clothe your family in designer styles for less than garage-sale prices.

- Many public schools take part in the federally funded National School Lunch Program that provides free or reduced-cost school lunches (and in some cases even breakfasts) to those who qualify. Visit www.fns.usda. gov/cnd/lunch or check with your child's school guidance counselor for more information on this program.

## Let Me Entertain You . . . on a Dime!

Movie tickets for three: $21. Summer camp: $600. Pizza and pop for a family of four: $40. If you're not cautious, entertaining kids can break the bank, or certainly put a huge dent in it. When it comes time to trade work for fun, try these ideas. You'll find that your family can save money *and* have a good time:

- Sending children to after-school activities and summer and school vacation camps can be a huge financial stress for single moms. Your local YMCA may offer reduced tuition and scholarships for income-eligible families. Many camps also offer scholarships or reduced tuitions based on financial need. Community centers and churches often host free vacation Bible schools and summer sports camps that are open to the general public.

- Your local library can also be a great resource. From using the Internet to borrowing books and movies, utilizing the public library can save you money. You may have to wait a few months to get a new release, but it would save you the cost of a $15 night at the movies. Libraries also usually have story-time hours, craft times, sing-a-longs and a host of other free events for the kids, as well as free seminars on relevant topics such as tax preparation and financial planning for adults.

- Take advantage of "early bird" specials. From eating dinner at a restaurant to attending a matinee performance, you can save a bit of money by beating the clock. Many children's programs and activities have "early bird" registration that provides savings for those who are quick to reserve their slot.

- Buy one, get one free. Be on the lookout for special promotions at your favorite restaurant and other venues. I know families who will only go to Friendly's on Wednesday nights, when kids eat free.

- BYOB. Lots of fast food places offer deals on $1.00 meals, but they make their money back on the drink sales! Beat the system by stocking up on bottled water, juices, teas or soft drinks at bargain prices, then grab a few of them before you go to the drive-thru. Or train your kids to enjoy the pure, clean taste of water (free if you ask for it in a cup), and save soft drinks for very special treats—that way, you'll save on eating out and dental bills!

## Housing Help

Most communities have a housing authority that can direct you to affordable housing and help you to determine what type of housing assistance you may qualify for. Habitat for Humanity (www.habitat.org) also helps families secure a home by offering selected eligible families a no-profit, no-interest loan.

Gas and electric companies often provide assistance to low-income families through reduced rates. Your local yellow pages (or Internet search engine) can direct you to your area service providers. Be sure to contact them directly to see if they offer heating and/or fueling assistance.

## Upgrading Your Skills or Going Back to School

Though many single moms imagine that there is no way they can afford to go back to school, it pays to visit your local college's financial aid counselor. Many women have been able to attend school full time, having gathered enough grants and scholarships (check out www.singlemom.com/RESOURCES/financialaid.htm) to equal what they'd be making if they were working instead. By upgrading your skills or getting a degree, you could increase your earning power and personal satisfaction for years to come. So don't toss out the possibility of returning to school without first talking to a sympathetic financial aid counselor at your local community college or university.

Tuition reimbursement is a great benefit that many companies are now offering to their employees. Finding a job that will put you through school is an awesome way to expand your skill set and your pocketbook. I know of a mom who works as a licensed radiology technician at her local hospital. In her field, she can become licensed in other modalities of radiology, such as CAT Scan and MRI, and significantly increase her salary by doing so—and all it costs her is a weekly class for 9 months, 160 hours in the clinic and a passing grade on her licensing exam. All the expenses (except her testing fee) are paid by her employer.

When job searching, you may also want to consider taking a position with a company that offers a sign-on bonus. Career Builder.com and Monster.com often advertise positions in a wide range of fields, from healthcare to computer programming, that offer a sizeable bonus if you sign on with a particular company. In fact, many companies base their offering bonus (and go above and beyond it) on the bonus you would forfeit at your current position by signing on with them.

## Emotional Hurdles

### Rejecting Shame

By now you're probably thinking to yourself, *If only taking advantage of the resources available to me were as easy as filling out a form.* The emotional strain that comes along with asking for help, and then accepting it, can be overwhelming.

Reaching out when you truly need help can be humbling. Having to admit that you can't provide for your child by yourself can evoke feelings of failure, guilt, shame, embarrassment and all sorts of other negative emotions. The fear of your child being teased because she gets free lunch; the eyes of the cashier glaring at you when you pay for your groceries with food stamps; or the thought of having to tell your child you can't afford a new pair of shoes can be enough to want to make you suffer in silence— and continue the downward spiral of robbing Peter to pay Paul.

If this is your current situation, it's important to realize that asking for and accepting help when you truly need it is *honorable*. It isn't easy, and often means thinking with your head, rather than your heart, but putting your family's needs before your own feelings is the first step toward financial freedom. The help is there for a reason, and if you put it to good use, you and your kids will contribute back into the system for years to come. So don't be a Lone Ranger mom—determine to swallow your pride and take every advantage of all government and charitable help you can find so that you can more quickly move toward total independence. One day, when you've received that diploma or are making a great salary, or perhaps when you marry again and no longer have to count every penny, you'll be able to "pay it forward" to other struggling single moms.

## Finding Forgiveness

Single mothers often want someone in their life with whom they can share the struggles and the joys of parenting. Someone to be there to help bear the financial burden when things get tight. Someone to come alongside and cheer when Charlie takes his first step or Anna says her first word.

With the intense burden of having to do it all on your own, as you bear the emotional, physical and financial aspects of parenting, and of having to rely on others for help when you can't, it's easy for resentment toward the MIA father of your child to creep in. Finding forgiveness is the key to freeing yourself from negative emotions. It can cleanse you from anger, bitterness and resentment. It can free you to heal and allow your children to heal.

Even doctors have begun to understand that forgiveness can truly heal the heart. Research indicates that those who are harboring unforgiveness display telltale stress signs: elevated heart rate, blood pressure and increased muscle tension.[6]

In the poignant movie *Stepmom,* the divorced mom played by Susan Sarandon struggles to forgive her ex-husband who left her for a younger woman (played by Julia Roberts). There's a defining moment in the movie when one of the children (who is starting to warm up to the new stepmom) feels her loyalties torn and says to her mother, "I'll hate her if you want me to." At this point, the mom realizes that unforgiveness and bitterness are not going to help any of them move onward and upward. For the sake of her children, she lays down the heavy mantle of bitterness.

If your ex-husband is still in the picture, no matter how much you may personally resent him for how he has hurt you in the marriage, if he is a good dad, you've got to bite your tongue and encourage your children to enjoy their relationship with him. Many men who do not make good husbands make excellent, or at least decent, fathers (or part-time dads). However difficult it may be, remind yourself that you are serving your children's future mental health and happiness by refraining from venting about him to them.

But what if he is a deadbeat dad? The sort that shows up on occasion and the kids love him, but he doesn't contribute financially to their wellbeing? Or what if he's in and out of their lives? The healthiest moms don't make excuses for the dad's bad behavior, but they don't throw stones at him either. The children will eventually see and know which parent is always there for them. If your ex is not paying child support, you can (and in most cases probably should) pursue legal channels to make him honor his financial obligations—but you don't have to involve the children in the details or verbally bash him.

One mom who found herself suddenly single shared her story with me:

> I was so hurt, angry and depressed after my husband left that it was really hard not to want my child to be on my side. But I would just tell myself that God would take care of me, God was the judge—and lean harder on Him than I've ever done before. If I hadn't had my faith, I would have been a total basket case. But I saw God provide for me and my children in amazing ways, and the more I focused on His provision and the less I focused on the unfairness of the divorce, the happier I was, and the healthier my children were. I was determined to get through this trial better and more beautiful, not bitter and ugly!

True forgiveness isn't contingent on repentance from the other person. It's about making the conscious decision to step down from being the judge and jury of someone else's life, and allowing God to handle the rest. It's no longer renting the space in your head to bitterness, revenge and painful ruminations. Someone once said that forgiveness is setting the prisoner free, then discovering that you were the prisoner. Forgiving someone releases you from being the victim and allows you to let go of the anger so that you have more room to be filled up with love—and are free to cultivate love as a way of life in your family.

Forgiving yourself is another important aspect in working toward healing your heart. You may feel guilty that you didn't do enough to make your marriage work or that you can't support your child on your own. Or if your husband died, you may harbor some regrets that you were not always the perfect wife. Or maybe you are suffering from shame and embarrassment from having a child out of wedlock.

Regardless of your circumstances, feeling guilty over long-passed mistakes is a waste of emotional energy. Instead, ask God to forgive you and believe that He does! Then do whatever you can to make amends to anyone you've hurt in your past. After that, move on! If a guilt-related thought pops up, just say to yourself, *I've already dealt with that and God has forgotten it.* Then visualize a stop sign and do not allow your mind to waste any more time on unfruitful thinking. You've got a life to live and kids to raise! You can't drive toward the next great adventure if you keep staring at the rearview mirror.

## Time Management

What happens when your child gets sick, you have to miss a day of work, the household chores pile up, you don't have the energy to make dinner (never mind tidy up) and the thought of having a moment to yourself seems an unrealistic dream? It's called *Overload*.

From taking a shower to making a phone call, even the smallest routines in the life of a single mother can be complicated. You've barely been in the shower long enough for the water to get warm when you hear a knock at the door and whines of "Mommy, Mommmyyy!" And you're not even out of the house yet. Next come the burdens of day-to-day tasks on top of a full-time job, tasks like carrying in the groceries from the car with your toddler in tow, helping with homework, putting the kids to bed night after night without backup from a partner. It all takes a toll.

What's a harried single mother to do? Here are some tips that have worked for other single moms I've known and interviewed:

- Carla sets her alarm so that she wakes up an hour or more before her kids in order to give herself a jump-start on the day. "This precious hour gives me a few valuable minutes to enjoy my cup of coffee and read an uplifting psalm in my Bible. It also provides enough time to take a shower, get dressed, prepare breakfast and get lunches made—without being summoned in three different directions. Then, once my kids get up, I'm ready and able to turn my attention to them."

• Stephanie incorporates a daily routine (which I suggested, based on her schedule and lifestyle) that she credits with turning her home from chaos into calm. Stephanie believes that mapping out her days and having a set time for taking baths, eating meals, going to bed and doing laundry—a load a day if she can—has helped her set her daily priorities so that she can work around them. She's found that laying out clothes (hers and the kids') the night before, having a set place where backpacks and shoes go, keeping an ongoing grocery list on the fridge, having a running to-do list and tidying up as she goes saves her a few hours over the course of a week.

• Linda eliminates craziness in the kitchen by keeping her pantry well stocked with the staples. She makes this suggestion to other single working moms: "Keep a loaf of bread in the freezer and always buy two gallons of milk and plenty of eggs at one time so that you won't have to make an emergency trip to the store." For tasty meals with minimal effort, she likes to Google "quick dinner ideas" for easy and fast entrées to add to her weekly repertoire. Linda prints out the promising recipes and adds them to a three-ring binder; then she highlights the ingredients to add to her shopping list

• Jessica shares this time-saver: "Utilizing online services gives you the flexibility to do things when they fit into your schedule." Paying your bills and even grocery shopping online (try www.peapod.com) can often save you money and time. If you're willing to do your research and check personal references, you can even find a local babysitter with the click of a mouse (check out www.sit tercity.com).

• Madison insists, "Having a backup plan in place for days when your child gets sick will let you fly on autopilot, rather than by the seat of your pants." She considers herself lucky to have family up the road, but when they were away on vacation and she got into a jam, she had a backup plan. Madison suggests, "Check with your employer to see if they have a policy for missing work due to a child's illness." Some employers offer sick care for their employee's children, where they pay the fee at a local facility that specializes in caring for mildly ill children. Others will allow you the flexibility to work from home. Your church may also be a resource for connecting with other mothers who help each other out in a pinch.

## Misconceptions and Myths

We've all overheard the whispers—if not in reality, then in the corners of our own worried minds.

"Statistically, he's going to be a failure, you know. That's what divorce does to kids."

"She must be a real witch if he left her."

"How sad . . . now Tommy is destined to be in a failed marriage, too."

"What a bad mother to work full time and leave someone else to raise her kids."

To set the record straight, *bad mothering makes a bad mother*. Not being a single mother. Not being a working mother. Not being a single working mother.

Now I don't think anyone would argue that the best place to raise a child is in a loving marriage, with both mother and father. In an ideal world without domestic abuse, death, alcoholism and extramarital affairs, the family unit as designed by God would still be universally intact—no exceptions.

But let me say, from personal experience: Don't let statistics tell you who and what your child is going to be. My parents were divorced, so, statistically speaking, I should be a failure. I certainly shouldn't be a happily married mom and parenting consultant. I also shouldn't be a college graduate or be living above the poverty line. I surely shouldn't be a published parenting author.

Each day I thank God that my single working mother looked to Him for my plans and purpose and trusted Him with my future. I encourage you to do the same. So many fabulous people were raised in single-parent homes! Oprah Winfrey was raised by her grandmother. Beautiful actress Halle Berry? Raised by a single mom. Naomi Judd raised two unique, talented and wonderful daughters alone. Ricky Henderson, the all-star baseball player, was raised without a dad in his life.

Remember, it's not who your kids *don't* have in their lives that matters, it is who they *do* have that makes a difference. Pick up the Bible and you'll read about all sorts of dysfunctional and broken families. But with God's grace, their trials made them even stronger and intensified their faith in the One who loved them, provided for them and gave them courage to face the future with hope.

## Forming a Support System

Single working mothers often feel as though their life is as shaky as a line of dominoes. They may have all the pieces lined up in a row—a job, childcare and transportation—but if one piece falls out of place, the rest of the dominoes topple over as well. Having a support system (with a backup plan) is essential to successfully navigating life as a single working mother. A support system is really a network of people that you can count on, a group of people you can trust.

Every person can't be everything to you, but if you take a close look around, you'll probably find that you are surrounded by people who can help here and there, now and then. I recommend that you make a list of these contacts, and ask them ahead of time if you could call on them in a minor emergency. Most people love to feel needed and are delighted to be asked to help out when you are in a bind.

For example, you may need two or three moms you can call to drop off or pick up your kids from school if you have a work or traffic emergency. Call them ahead of time and say something like, "Elaine, you are one of those moms I've really come to admire and trust. As a single mom, I need more emergency back-ups than the average married mom. So, I am wondering if you'd mind being one of the people I can put on my list to call if I should get waylaid at work and need someone to pick up Tom after school and keep him until I can get there. And I'd be happy to return the favor. Could we exchange phone numbers just in case?"

As Dean Martin crooned, "Everybody needs somebody sometime." This is probably truer for single working mothers than it is for most people. Because you are flying solo in the parenting cockpit, it's important to get the much-needed support that will help you to land your child safely into adulthood.

## Family Ties

For many single mothers, relocating near extended family provides a great source of support. Aunts, uncles and cousins can give your kids some rich experiences, and male relatives can help give your son some much-needed male bonding if his father is out of the picture or only visits occasionally. If your parents are retired, they are often at a place in life where they have plenty of free time and welcome the opportunity to bond more closely with your kids. Your dad and your son may both benefit when they help each other out with the "man stuff" around your house. Though you'll want to be sensitive to your parents' need for privacy and alone time, remember that most people—especially retired and older people—need to feel needed. It's good for them, emotionally and physically!

## Making Friends into Family!

Others moms, due to family strains or financial circumstances, aren't able to relocate close to relatives. If you find yourself in this situation, it's important that you turn to your close friends and your church family for support. One mom shared her inspiring story of making friends into family:

> My best friend and I became known to our kids as their "second moms." When we both ended up single, we moved next door to each other in the same apartment building. I can't tell you what a relief it was for both of us to be the backup mom to each other's children in any number of circumstances. When I was running late, my kids could walk to their second mom's kitchen and grab some dinner. When my friend was out of town for a weekend to care for an ailing mother, I was able to be the second mom to her brood. I honestly don't know what we'd have done without each other. I highly recommend that a single mom foster a close friendship with another single mom she likes and admires, and consider moving into the apartment complex or neighborhood that she lives in. Then the two of them can make a pact to be there for each other and each other's kids.

Check out community or church programs that are geared toward single parents. Some even have support groups for single moms that facilitate connections between other Christian single moms and host special events for single-parent families. It's such a healthy experience for your kids to spend time with other kids who are also from single-parent homes—not to mention, it's a boon to you. If you find the right single-parenting group, it can become a family unto itself. Support groups for single parents can be great resources for recipes, tips for single-parent-friendly outings, entertainment and vacation ideas, friendships, baby-sitting co-ops and hand-me-downs for the kids.

Don't underestimate the variety of help that can be found in your local church, support group or community center. For example, the attorney who attends your church may not be able to answer your specific questions, but she may be able to refer you to an attorney who does pro-bono work for single moms. Ask, ask, ask. One little-known fact about human nature is that most people *love* to be asked for advice. It makes them feel good and helps you out at the same time. It's a win-win!

As long as you keep a good balance of give and take, friends will be delighted to help. Making the effort to form lots of friendships keeps you from overtaxing one particular friend. Feather your single-parenting nest with as many friend-ships as you can possibly fit into your busy life, and nourish the friendships that are mutually supportive and beneficial to your children. When you are tempted to have a pity party be-cause you don't have a husband to snuggle with on cold evenings, you can put on a pot of chili, call up a couple of sin-gle parents and ask them over for dinner (they can bring corn-bread and a salad!), and watch a movie while the kids play a board game. Create your own unconventional, rag-tag family! Everyone benefits.

Joining an online support forum for single working moth-ers can be a great place to share tips and experiences (as well as have that occasional venting session!). Visiting websites dedi-cated to single moms (such as www.acupofjoy.org) will provide you with great resources and inspirational stories from others who have walked in similar shoes. In times of struggle, these brief testimonies can provide the dose of encouragement you need to push on.

My mother used to say to me, "Michelle, if you don't ask, you don't get." It's really true. If you don't share your needs with others, they won't be met. Be open and honest with those around you. You may be surprised with the results.

## SCENE 10: TAKE 2
### Parent-Teacher Conference

**Mrs. Haskins** (*to Kathy, the mother of her student Isaac*): I've asked you to come in today because I am concerned with Isaac's attendance record.

**Kathy:** Yes, we've been having some trouble getting things together in the morning.

**Mrs. Haskins:** Are you aware that he's been absent 4 times this semester, late 18 out of the last 60 days of school and 7 times been the last student on the school grounds—an hour after the closing bell rang—and the vice principal was unable to reach you?

**Kathy:** I'm sorry. I didn't realize it's been that much; I'm doing the best I can.

**Mrs. Haskins** (*curt and clearly unimpressed with her response*): Kathy, I'm not sure you understand the severity of the situation. If this continues, Isaac will be in jeopardy of not being promoted to the sixth grade. He's reached the maximum of tardy days permitted per school year—and we are barely halfway through the second term. (*Then, seeing the look on Kathy's face, Mrs. Haskins changes her* *tone.*) Is there something I can do to help you get him here on time? Is everything at home okay?

**Kathy** (*upset and attempting to hold back tears*): I need to work two jobs to make ends meet. I deliver the morning paper before school, and if I'm running late, Isaac ends up being late. Then I waitress during the day and my shift ends when the school bell rings. I get here as soon as I can—and the day I was *really* late, my car died. I had to catch a ride just to get here. I really think I need some help. I just have nowhere to turn, no one to depend on.

**Mrs. Haskins** (*sympathetically while touching her shoulder*): Oh, Kathy, I'm sorry. I didn't know all this was going on. Please keep me informed and let me know what I can do to help. I can get Vice Principal Thomas in the loop so that we can find a way to help you. You know, the school has some resources that may be of assistance. I know we offer limited transportation, have a carpool connection, and I think we even have a list of available sitters and tutors from the local college who work in exchange for credits toward the experience requirements for their coursework. Let's go down to the guidance office and see what information we can get together.

**Kathy:** Thank you, Anne. I'm at the point now where I'll take any help I can get. I wish I had asked the school for help sooner. I feel a bit better already just by sharing what's been going on.

**Mrs. Haskins:** We're here to help. We'll figure this out together.

## HOW DID KATHY GET THE HELP SHE NEEDED FOR HER SON?

- *She was honest about her situation.* It is better to be open and honest about what is going on rather than to suffer in silence.

- *She asked for help.* "If you don't ask, you don't get." People can't help you if they don't know you're in need.

- *She was willing to accept help.* It can be hard to accept a helping hand. Giving back to others can make accepting help a bit easier.

- *She was able to put her pride aside to get the help that she and her son needed.* Don't let your feelings dictate your actions. Even though it is hard to ask for help, sharing your needs is the right thing to do. Someday, you will be in a better position and can "pay forward" the benevolence you now need to make it through this tough time.

- *She tapped into the support of people already around her.* The people around you already can be your greatest resources. Be sure to network with those already in your daily circle.

---

**Q:** *My daughter is in Scouts, and they are having a father-daughter dance. Unfortunately, her father is not in the family picture anymore. She hasn't said anything, but I can tell she is really upset. What can I do?*

**A:** Ask her grandfather, an uncle or a close family friend to stand in and help make this a truly memorable event for your daughter.

*Q:* One of the most difficult things about being a single mom to an eight-year-old boy is dealing with public bathrooms. Any advice?

**A:** Ideally, a family restroom or separate handicap bathroom would be your best bet, but if that's not possible, I think that it is acceptable to bring your son into the women's bathroom with you until he's 9 or 10. Although kids may be able to handle using the bathroom on their own well before then, they may not be mature enough to handle an emergency, should it arise. When making a decision about whether or not you should allow your child to use the public restroom by himself, take into account where you are. Using the bathroom at a local restaurant with a single stall and where you can stand outside, is much different from sending him solo into the public restroom at a busy sports arena. Sending your child into a public restroom with a friend or buddy adds a measure of safety as well.

*Q:* My twins want me to be involved at school, but because I need to work, I am not able to volunteer for school-related functions as much as the stay-at-home moms. They now play in a weekend soccer league and want me to coach. I don't know a thing about soccer, but I don't want to let them down anymore. Any ideas?

**A:** I have fond memories of my single working mom coaching my sports team. My advice: Get a good book, learn all the rules and offer to be an assistant coach. Pair up with someone who has experience in coaching kids' soccer, and give it your best shot. Even bringing drinks or snacks to practice for the team will be a valuable contribution that your kids won't forget!

*Q:* I've been divorced for three years, and I've recently started to date. Any time the man I am seeing picks me up at the house, my four-year-old cries and the babysitter ends up calling me because she can't calm him down. I need to have a life, but I don't want to upset my child.

**A:** One of the easiest ways to correct this issue is to not have your date come to your house. Until a relationship becomes truly serious, the kids should not be involved. If after a lengthy courtship the relationship looks like it's going in the permanent direction, introduce your son to him slowly, on neutral ground. Be clear to whomever you are dating that your kids come first. Then be sure to remind your children—often!—that they were not the cause of your divorce. When the kids see that things are getting serious between you and your boyfriend, naturally they will begin to ask, "Is that going to be my new daddy?" The best answer, if your ex is a good father, is, "No one could ever replace your daddy. But [insert name] is our good friend, and maybe someday if we decide to marry, he'll be my husband and your stepfather."

**Q:** *I am a single mom and money is tight. My daughter just started to notice that I buy her clothes from second-hand stores. She told me she's embarrassed and doesn't want me to shop there anymore.*

**A:** Now is a great time to introduce your child to the concept of a budget. Sit down with her and draw a pie chart that shows how you spend your income. You don't need to use numbers; the size of the slice should convey the message. Explain how much you budget to spend on clothing and show her some store ads. Let her know that for every one brand-new designer item at full price, you can buy five gently used designer items. Maybe you can come to a compromise: Allow her to do additional household tasks to earn her own money that she can spend on a new article of clothing, or maybe you can shop together on eBay where she can have some input without having to "be seen" shopping thriftily.

**Q:** *I am a single mom to a seven-year-old boy, and I'm already beginning to wonder who will have "the talk" with him when the time comes.*

**A:** Ideally, a grandfather or an uncle could step up to the plate and share in this important part of the growing-up process. If you go that route, have a talk with your chosen delegate to be sure that you are on the same page when it comes to what and how much information is to be shared. If you really feel like you are on your own, Jim Burns, a trusted Christian family expert and radio personality, has two new books and an audio resource for parents and kids to help guide you. The book for parents is called *Teaching Your Children Healthy Sexuality* and the book for kids ages 9-12 is titled *The Purity Code*. The audio resource ("The Purity Code") is made up of interviews with trusted youth experts who talk about puberty, sex, relationships, and much more. Also, a book by Grace H. Kettermen titled *Teaching Your Child About Sex* is a great resource.

*Q:* *I am a single working mom-to-be. I am nervous about giving birth because I won't have a man there to support me. Would it be weird to ask someone to be there with me?*

**A:** Absolutely not! Your mom, aunt or sister would probably love the opportunity to support you through the birthing process. Even a best friend who's given birth can be an amazing birthing partner. The main things to consider are: *Is this a person I can really trust? Is this someone who will be my advocate? Will this person respect my wishes? Is this person supportive of me?* If you can answer yes to these questions, then you've probably picked the right partner. If you feel like there is no one in your close circle that could help you, consider hiring a doula to support and encourage you during your birth experience.

# MICHELLE'S SUPER SOLUTIONS

## *A* to *Z* Tips for the Most Common Dilemmas Working Mothers Face

In my time spent working alongside busy moms, I've come to appreciate how really strapped for time today's working mothers can be. So as a way to creatively streamline and review the information in this book, I've created my own glossary of tips. They are organized as a quick-reference tool that should get any working mother back on track when the craziness of doing it all has temporarily derailed her.

## A

**Access help**—Is there a source of help that you may be overlooking? After reading this book, list all the areas of your life in which you are feeling particularly bogged down; then under each area, list ideas for ways you might enlist the help of others to ease your stress: your husband, the kids, relatives, friends, community resources, housekeeping, once-a-month cooking, and so on.

**Allow for a learning curve**—Successfully implementing new ideas and trying new routines take time. Give yourself and your family time to become familiar with the newness, and allow ample opportunity to tweak things to meet the needs of your specific situation.

**A place for everything**—Baskets in the hall closet for shoes, a spot to hang the backpacks, a special storage bin for library books. Having a designated place for personal items allows the kids to get involved in helping with tidying up, and keeps you from frantic last-minute searches for missing items.

## B

**Backup care and beyond**—Have two levels of backup childcare always available. When the kids are home from school sick, know whom you can call—and know whom you can call if the first attempt fails.

**Baskets**—Baskets are a multipurpose miracle! You can find a basket in every shape and size, ready to hold everything from your arsenal of loose pens in your junk drawer to medications you need to store high in the top of the closet (out of reach of the kiddos).

**Believe in your decisions**—If you've made the right decision for you and your family, that's all that matters. Trust your motherly instincts, and leave naysayers to blow their advice into the wind. Focus on where you're going and how you're going to get there.

## C

**Caregiver communication**—Having open and honest communication at all times with your caregiver is the key to any caregiving arrangement. Praise your provider when things are going well, and bring things up as soon as you notice that they are going not-so-well.

**Childcare choices**—Being confident in your childcare choice is the number-one tip working moms give. Knowing your caretaker well and knowing that you can completely trust him or her will alleviate lots of anxiety.

**Current calendar**—When appointments are made (or cancelled), update your calendar immediately, and be sure to notify those who are affected by the schedule changes.

# D

**Defer**—Never feel pressured to commit to something when you're not sure that you can do it. Managing kids, home and work can get hairy, and an "I'll have to get back to you" is a much better choice than making a commitment that you won't be able to keep.

**Delegate**—Can your kids take out the trash? Can your husband take Saturday soccer duty? Look for opportunities to ask others to help.

**Do for you**—I can't overstate the importance of taking care of yourself and doing things just for you. A happy mom really does make for a happy family.

# E

**Easy access to your most needed things**—Keep what you need handy. A binder in the kitchen that has frequently used phone numbers, lists of current prescriptions of family members, office contacts and home-repair service numbers will give you a one-stop shop for information that you often can't find when you really need it.

**Eat healthy**—Take time to eat regularly scheduled snacks and meals. Chasing kids and managing home and office can sometimes leave you running around like a chicken with your head cut off. Take time to stop and eat something nourishing so that you can get the energy boost that you need. If you are one of those highly focused women who sometimes forget to eat, pencil "snack time" into your Dayrunner to be sure you get the nutrients that you need.

**Enjoy the little things**—Taking a few minutes to smell the roses in your life can cultivate an attitude of appreciation and gratefulness, which reduces stress and serves as an instant attitude adjustment when things aren't going as you'd wish.

# F

**Family time**—Set aside one night a week for doing something together and celebrating your family unit. Whether it be a game night, a walk around the block or a weekly devotional, be sure to take time to reconnect as a family.

**Find time for you!**—Take a few minutes for yourself each day to recharge your batteries. Whether it be taking a bath or reading a book, set aside a few minutes to do something for you. I've said it before, but it's worth saying again and again and again . . . and again!

**Forget about it**—When everything seems to be falling apart before your very eyes, take a deep breath, regroup, get back on track and leave the past where it belongs: behind you.

# G

**Get to the gym**—Hit the gym after work or take a brisk walk on your lunch break. A bit of exercise helps relieve stress and is good for the body—and the soul.

**God is in control**—Always remember that God loves you and has your best interests at heart; He is in complete control of your situation, regardless of the circumstances or the way things may seem right now.

**Guilt-free is the way to be!**—The number-one emotion working moms face is guilt. If you're doing what's best for you and yours, that's what truly matters. Get a cup of cocoa, put your feet up and flip back to the "guilt section" in this book—you'll quickly remember that guilt-free really is the way to be.

# H

**Happy faces**—When you're feeling overwhelmed or frustrated, smile! Like that old saying goes, "Frown and you frown alone, smile and the whole world smiles with you."

**Have a day set aside for errands**—Set aside a block of time one day of the week, just get to the store, the post office and to run any other errands. Knowing that you have a set time to do these things will eliminate the stress that comes from trying to cram just one more thing into your already hectic workday.

**Hire help**—Whether you hire a college student to run your errands, invest in a bi-monthly housekeeper or employ a dog walker, hire out some of your most loathed and time-consuming household tasks if your budget allows.

# I

**Indulge!**—Maybe it's expensive French soap, salon-quality shampoo or some chocolate fudge from your favorite confectionary. Whatever your favorite little indulgence, splurge when you can on something that makes you feel special.

**Invest in your childcare choice**—The importance of having a relationship with your caregiver cannot be overstated. Take time to really know your caregiver (ask how her weekend was, how her classes are going, and so on), give a bonus or a gift when your caregiver goes above and beyond the call of duty and really listen when she talks to you about your child.

**In and Out boxes**—These are keys for smooth communication with the outside world. Give each member of the family an In and Out box that holds school notices, to-do task lists and scheduling requests. This eliminates chasing down paperwork that could otherwise easily go missing.

# J

**Jot a list**—Always have a pen and pad handy so that when you think of something you need or need to do, you can write it down immediately rather than risk forgetting it.

**Journal**—Keeping a journal can be a great way to vent, record cherished memories or keep track of changes in your family. Pick up a spiral bound notebook, keep it by your bed and jot down things that make you laugh, make you cry or just simply leave you confused.

**Just ask**—If there is an area in your life in which you need some help, resist the urge to try to do everything by yourself—ask for help. You may find that people are willing and ready to lend a hand, but they haven't wanted to "interfere" by offering to assist.

# K

**Keep going**—When the going gets tough, hold your head up and press on! Remember, inch by inch, anything is a cinch!

**Keep up with things as you go**—Cleaning the dishes as you cook, putting the laundry away as it's folded and picking up the playroom when the kids are done playing all save you from coming back to a mess later, when you probably won't have time to clean it up.

**Kids can help, too!**—Give your kids age-appropriate chores to do around the house. Kids want to feel part of the family unit and to feel valued for contributing to the family's wellbeing. Whether you have them tidy their room, feed the dog or babysit a sibling, enlist the help of the kids in day-to-day household operations.

# L

**Lend a hand**—Any good relationship is a balance of give and take, so be sure that if you have a friend or parent who's been helping you out, take time to return the favor.

**Let go and let God**—Remember who is really in control. Know that God is a good God and only has your best at heart. When things get to be too much, offer up a prayer and cast your burdens on Him who will be faithful to meet your needs.

**Live by lists**—Lists are vital to working mothers. Having a daily to-do list helps you visualize and prioritize what really needs to get done. Checking things off as you go gives you a boost of confidence as you see what you can accomplish in just one day!

## M

**Marathon cooking days**—Consider taking one day a week to cook up and freeze casseroles, lasagnas or stews. That way you'll have quick and easy meals that you can defrost in the morning and pop in the oven when you get home.

**Meal-time magic**—Have a set time when meals are served. Getting everyone together for dinner (before they've reached the point of starvation!) is the key to staying connected in our busy world.

**Morning management**—Have a morning routine that allows you enough time to get ready to face the day. Have a set time for everyone's shower, breakfast and departure; then give warning reminders when time is running short.

## N

**New to you**—Try shopping at consignment shops for school clothes, or take advantage of hand-me-downs. Get a group of gals together and have a seasonal swap of kids' clothing.

**Nighttime for the next day**—Prepare what you can for the next day the night before. Laying out clothes and packing lunches at night can save you valuable morning time.

**No is a good word**—Don't be afraid to say no when you can't meet a request. Look for alternative ways to help that fit within your personal constraints.

# O

**Once-over**—Each night before everyone hits the hay, have your family help you give the house a quick once-over so that you can wake up to clear pathways and uncluttered tabletops and countertops.

**Organize**—Implementing an organizational system can restore order to an otherwise chaotic environment. Color coding closets and cleaning out the fridge weekly allow you to see what you have and what you need.

**Original ideas**—Outside the box can often be where the solution to your problem is found. Look for creative ideas that may work in the situation you're struggling with.

# P

**Plan in advance**—Whenever you can, take time to think things through and plan out your day in advance. While you are lying in bed in the morning, just after the alarm has gone off, spend a few minutes thinking about your day and what you need to get done. A little reflection can make you much more productive.

**Prayer and petition**—Take a moment each morning to thank God for the day and to lay your requests before Him.

**Prioritize your day**—Know what can wait and what can't. Take your handy to-do list and group things by what has to be done today, what has to be done this week and what can be put off until later.

# Q

**Quick fix**—Tape a list of your favorite 21 quick-fix meals, along with their ingredients and recipes, to your pantry door so that you always have what you need to feed the troops in a jiffy.

**Quiet time**—Teach your kids (and yourself!) to appreciate time alone. Reading books, praying or knitting are all quiet-time activities that can be enjoyed without the company of others.

**Quiz the kids**—Run through "What happens if . . . ?" scenarios with your kids. "What do you do if you miss the bus?" "What should you do if Mom was supposed to pick you up at three and she's late?" Talking through various scenarios will prepare your kids for how to handle things that may come up unexpectedly.

# R

**Rock on with routines**—Everyone operates best when she knows what to expect and what is expected from her. From bedtime to school drop-off and homework time, having a routine in place will help everyone to accomplish what needs to get done.

**Roll with the flow**—Have a few calming phrases to tell yourself when you begin to feel over-hurried and harried. *All is well* and *Peace, be still* work well for me.

**Rolodex to the ready**—Keep a list of important phone numbers and contact information with you at all times. A small notebook in your pocketbook is a handy way to store school personnel numbers, caregiver numbers, backup caregiver numbers, and so on.

# S

**School spirit**—Even the busiest of working moms can find a way to help out in their child's school. Whether compiling the class contact list, baking cookies or helping the teacher with a special project, there are always ways to help outside of being in the classroom (which is when you need to be at work). Ask the teacher what she needs, and sure as sugar she'll find a task that works for you and your schedule.

**Separation anxiety**—Every child, at some time or another, goes through a phase when they don't want to be away from Mommy (my baby girl's hitting this phase early at four months!). If you are confident in your caregiving arrangement, show your child your confidence by being positive and keeping goodbyes short, sweet and final. Calling the caregiver from the car to see if Charlie has settled in is a much better option than peeking in and getting caught!

**Simplify**—Eliminate the unnecessary, and look for the simplest way to accomplish what needs to get done.

# T

**Thrive on time**—High School Marching Band 101: *To be early is to be on time.* Strive to be a few minutes early for appointments. That way, if something comes up or if you run into traffic, you will still be on time.

**Time off**—Utilize your personal days as emotional wellness days. Try to take a day every few months—a day when the kids are in school—and be good to yourself. This eliminates babysitting costs and the stress of finding a caregiver—and gives you much-needed personal time for you and you alone (or you and your husband, if he can take a day off, too!). But *shhh!* Don't tell the kids!

**Transitions**—Kids deal with transitions best when they know what to expect and know that you are confident in what comes next. Prepare your kids to switch gears by winding down activities with a five-minute warning and by having them participate in getting ready for what comes next.

## U

**Unconditionally love yourself**—At the end of the day, love yourself for who God has made you to be—not for what you've done or accomplished.

**Understand that you're doing a lot**—Realize that your plate is full and cut yourself some slack. Take time to pat yourself on the back for all that you are accomplishing, and set small, realistic goals for where you want to improve.

**Utilize the Internet**—From grocery shopping to shoe shopping, use the Internet to save time. With the click of the mouse, you can get what you need and have it delivered directly to your door. Added bonus: If you shop in the evening, you can shop without the kids and not have to pay for a babysitter!

## V

**Vacation**—Make the best use of your vacation days. Try to schedule some of your time around your kids' activities—maybe a week off during their break between school and camp—or use days so that you can attend the school Christmas pageant or the next fieldtrip.

**Variables in children**—Remember, fair doesn't always mean equal. Realize that each child is different and has different needs; parenting kids isn't one-size-fits-all. Strive to provide each child with what he needs to succeed.

**Victorious**—You are victorious! I'll say it again: Celebrate the little things you've accomplished. It will give you the motivation you need to push through the hard times and keep moving forward.

# W

**Weather the storms together**—Be open and honest with your spouse about what's going on. Remember that there is no *I* in "teamwork" and raising a family is a joint effort. If you are a single mom, this means reaching out to your network to get the support that you need—you're not in this alone.

**Weekly meal-planning**—Take time to pre-plan a week's worth of dinners. Write down the menu and put it on the fridge door. Make your grocery list based on this menu. When you see "Crock-Pot Roast" for Wednesday night, it will remind you to thaw the meat on Tuesday night and pop it in the Crock-Pot before work on Wednesday morning. Then remember that Boston Market takeout counts as a home-cooked meal. (Okay, you didn't cook it—but somebody did.)

**Weigh the pros and the cons**—Before making a decision, take the time to weigh out the pros and the cons. Because something looks easy in the moment, it doesn't really mean it's the best choice for the long haul.

# X

**X-rated**—Remember that what goes into your family members' ears and eyes sits and cooks in their minds until it finds some way to come back out. Monitor your kids' Internet use, video game use and movie selections carefully, and be sure their choices align with your family's moral standards.

**X-ray vision**—Take the time to look into what your child is trying to communicate. Her body language, eye contact (or lack thereof), demeanor and tone all provide insight into her true feelings.

**Xerox copy**—Photocopy your important documents and keep them in one place. Birth certificates and immunization records are often needed to complete school and camp enrollment, and securing replacement documentation can be a nightmare.

# Y

**Yes is yes and no is no**—Sometimes we give others too much information. Let your yes be yes and your no be no. Avoid going into long-winded explanations when they really aren't needed. This is especially true when you want to avoid getting swayed by someone to change your mind. A clear yes or no allows no room for negotiation.

**Yuck it up!**—The family that laughs together is a family that can handle the challenge of two working parents or a single working mother.

**Yummy tummy time**—Nothing gets a kid in the appreciative, talkative, "want to spend time with family" mood like a surprise treat. If you need a family-time fix, an ice-cream sundae party will surely get everyone gathered around the table.

# Z

**Zero tolerance**—If there are things in your life that just push you over the edge, insist on a zero-tolerance policy. Swear words? Name-calling? Hitting? Whatever you don't want in your home, set clear guidelines and have definitive consequences for breaking them. This eliminates confusion and sets up clear expectations for your kids (and your caregiver).

**Zip it**—Put negativity under wraps. It can be tempting to focus on the negative when things aren't going as planned, but stay positive and keep negative thoughts (and sometimes people) at arm's length. Thank God for what He's doing and ask for help when you need it.

**Zoom through the easy stuff first**—When you have a list of tasks that need to be accomplished, it is often helpful to breeze through the least time-consuming first. It builds your confidence, shows you what you've accomplished and gives you enough of a push to tackle the more time-consuming items on your list.

# WRAP-UP!

Give yourself a hand! You've tackled yet another task on your never-ending working mother to-do list. If you've finished this book, my hope is that you take away some practical tips and new ideas for how to navigate working motherhood. It's my hope that with my advice and encouragement, "doing it all" has become just a bit easier.

I know we've covered a lot in these pages, but perhaps a few chapters have already helped you improve a particular situation or transition into a new phase. Maybe you've got the confidence to present your boss with a perfectly tailored maternity-leave plan or you've solidified a childcare solution that works like a magnificently tuned machine. Or maybe you've felt like a friend has come alongside you and given you the encouragement you need to be secure in your decision to return to work.

Things have changed a bunch for me since I began work on this book. Just as soon as I finished the Maternity Leave section of this book, my husband, Jeff, and I learned that we were expecting our first child! Of course this led to lots of tweaking in the pregnancy and maternity chapters of this book and provided me with ample opportunity to apply the tricks and tips to my personal work situation. For that reason alone, I'm confident that you have a pretty good book in your hands (but then again, I guess I'm biased!).

So I leave you with my support, prayers, encouragement and hope as you continue on your journey. As for me, I think I'll get crackin' on my next book, which I'm sure will be filled with new discoveries and plenty of laughs: *From Here to Maternity: What One Nanny Always Thought She Knew Until She Had a Child of Her Own.*

# ENDNOTES

**Chapter 1: The Mother Load**

1. Abigail Tuttle O'Keeffe, "It's Not What Mothers Do But the 'Reasons' That They Do It: Maternal Reasons for Employment Decisions and Mothers' Well-Being," presented at the Biennial Meeting of the Society for Research in Child Development in Minneapolis, MN, April 2001. http://eric.ed.gov/ERICWebPortal/Home.portal?_nfpb=true&ERICExtSearch_SearchValue_0=what+mothers+do&searchtype=basic&ERICExtSearch_SearchType_0=ti&_pageLabel=RecordDetails&objectId=0900019b800c5ec1&accno=ED454990&_nfls=false (accessed October 2008).

**Chapter 2: Maternity Leave 101**

1. "Pregnancy Discrimination Charges: FY 1997 – FY 2007," U.S. Equal Employment Opportunity Commission. http://www.eeoc.gov/stats/pregnanc.html (accessed October 2008).
2. "Sexual Harassment Charges: FY 1997 – FY 2007," U.S. Equal Employment Opportunity Commission. http://www.eeoc.gov/stats/harass.html (accessed October 2008).
3. "Facts About Pregnancy Discrimination," U.S. Equal Employment Opportunity Commission. http://www.eeoc.gov/facts/fs-preg.html (accessed October 2008).
4. "Pregnancy Discrimination," a publication of the New Mexico Commission on the Status of Women. http://www.womenscommission.state.nm.us/Publications/Pregnancy%20Discrimination%20brochure.pdf (accessed October 2008).
5. "Family and Medical Leave Act," U.S. Department of Labor Wage and Hour Division. http://www.dol.gov/esa/whd/fmla/ (accessed October 2008).
6. Amy Zintl, "How Does Your State Measure Up on Maternity Leave?" Parents.com. http://www.parents.com/pregnancy/my-life/maternity-paternity-leave/how-does-your-state-measure-up-on-maternity-leave/ (accessed October 2008).
7. "The Basics of Short Term Disability Insurance," Insure.com, Sept. 24, 2007. http://info.insure.com/disability/shorttermdisability.html (accessed October 2008).

**Chapter 3: Exhaustion, Cravings, Crying, Nausea and Nesting on the Job**

1. "75 Percent of Women Indulge Food Cravings But Only 8 Percent Reach for Healthy Substitutes," Market Wire, May 2005. http://findarticles.com/p/articles/mi_pwwi/is_200505/ai_n13644886 (accessed November 2008).

**Chapter 4: Leaving Your Precious Bundle in Loving Arms**

1. Dr. T. Berry Brazelton, M.D., cited on NAEYC Accreditation website, www.rightchoiceforkids.org.

**Chapter 5: Got Milk?**

1. "Breastfeeding and the Use of Human Milk," American Academy of Pediatrics Policy Statement, *Pediatrics,* vol. 115, no. 2, February 2005, pp. 496-506. http://aappolicy.aappublications.org/cgi/content/full/pediatrics;115/2/496#R123 (accessed November 2008).
2. Michelle Carnesecca, RN, IBCLC, "Mother's Hunger While Breastfeeding," October 2, 2008. http://en.allexperts.com/q/Breastfeeding-1764/2008/10/mother-hunger-breastfeeding.htm (accessed November 2008).

**Chapter 7: Summer Care, Backup Care and Everything-in-Between Care**

1. Paul Bannister, "Summer Camp Prices Vary Widely," Bankrate.com, March 16, 2006.

http://www.bankrate.com/brm/news/advice/20040223b1.asp (accessed November 2008).

## Chapter 10: Single Mom, Double Duty

1. "U.S. Divorce Statistics," Divorce Magazine.com. http://www.divorcemag.com/statistics/statsUS.shtml (accessed November 2008).

2. "Economic News Release: Families with Own Children: Employment Status of Parents by Age of Youngest Child and Family Type, 2006-07 Annual Averages," U.S. Bureau of Labor Statistics. http://www.bls.gov/news.release/famee.t04.htm (accessed November 2008).

3. Dr. Mary Gatta, "Increasing Access to Education and Skills Training for Low-Income Single Mothers: Online Learning as Training Policy," Rutgers Center for Women and Work at the School of Management and Labor Relations. http://www.itwd.rutgers.edu/PDF/Brief-OnlineLearningProgram.pdf (accessed November 2008).

4. "Federal Minimum Wage Increase 2007, 2008, & 2009," Labor Law Center.com. http://www.laborlawcenter.com/t-federal-minimum-wage.aspx?gclid=CKuVv6n74YwCFRYhgAodYy6f0g (accessed November 2008).

5. "The 2007 HHS Poverty Guidelines: One Version of the [U.S.] Federal Poverty Measure," United States Department of Health and Human Services. http://aspe.hhs.gov/poverty/07poverty.shtml (accessed November 2008).

6. Eileen O'Connor, "Forgiveness Heals the Heart, Research Hints," CNN.com, May 20, 1999. http://www.cnn.com/HEALTH/9905/20/forgiveness/ (accessed November 2008).

# ABOUT THE AUTHOR

MICHELLE LaROWE is the 2004 International Nanny Association Nanny of the Year and is the author of the *Nanny to the Rescue!* parenting series and *Working Mom's 411*. Michelle holds a Bachelor of Science degree in chemistry and a certificate in pastoral studies and has spent more than a decade as a professional nanny and parenting consultant. She is an active member of the nanny community, has served on the board of directors and as vice president of the International Nanny Association, and is also a proud member of Christian Nannies. Michelle has received citations and congratulations for her dedication to improving the quality of in-home childcare from Massachusetts Governor Mitt Romney and from President George W. Bush. She is regularly called on by the media as a nanny expert and has appeared on television (700 Club, NECN, FOX), has been featured in print (*USA Today, Boston Globe, Better Homes and Gardens*) and is a regular columnist for several magazines, including *TWINS* magazine and *Families Online Magazine*. She and her husband, Jeff, reside in a seaside village of Cape Cod with their daughter, Abigail.

# ALSO BY MICHELLE LAROWE

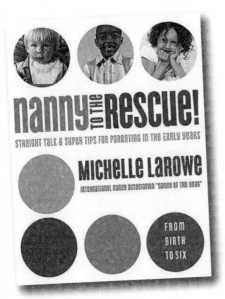

**NANNY TO THE RESCUE!**
From Birth to Six
(Nashville, TN: Thomas Nelson, 2006)
ISBN-10: 0849-91232-6
ISBN-13: 978-0849-91232-0

**NANNY TO THE RESCUE AGAIN!**
From Six to Twelve
(Nashville, TN: Thomas Nelson, 2006)
ISBN-10: 0849-91244-X
ISBN-13: 978-0849-91244-3

WWW.MICHELLELAROWE.COM